W9-BFR-398

Refilling
the
Jars

FINDING HOPE AFTER ADULTERY

by
Neil & Noline Rhodes

EBED

PUBLICATIONS

In love, serve one another

Special thanks to Mike and Marilyn Phillipps, our friends for life, for their love, encouragement, and help in writing this book.

Refilling the Jars: Finding Hope After Adultery
Copyright © 1996, 1998 by Neil and Noline Rhodes
ALL RIGHTS RESERVED

Contents and/or cover may not be reproduced in whole or in part without the express written consent of the publisher.

Scriptural references are from the New King James Version of the Bible, © copyright 1979, 1980, 1982 by Thomas Neslon, Inc., Nashville, Tennessee, unless otherwise noted. References marked "NIV" are from the New International Version of the Bible, © copyright 1973, 1978, 1984 by International Bible Society, Colorado Springs, Colorado. References marked "KJV" are from the Authorized King James Version of the Bible. References marked AMPLIFIED are from the Amplified Bible, © copyright 1987 by the Zondervan Corporation and the Lockman Foundation, La Habra Foundation, California.

EBED Publications is a division of The McDougal Foundation, Inc., a non-profit Maryland corporation dedicated to spreading the Gospel of Jesus Christ to as many people as possible in the shortest time possible.

First Printing: 1996
Second Printing: 1998

Published by:

EBED Publications
P.O. Box 3595
Hagerstown, MD 21742-3595

ISBN 1-884369-31-6

Printed in the United States of America

Dedication

I dedicate this book to my loving wife Noline who stood by me through all my trials.

He who finds a wife finds a good thing,
And obtains favor from the Lord.

Proverbs 18:22 NKJ

God's warnings regarding adultery:

For the commandment is a lamp,
And the law a light;
Reproofs of instruction are the way of life,
To keep you from the evil woman,
From the flattering tongue of a seductress.
Do not lust after her beauty in your heart,
Nor let her allure you with her eyelids.
For by means of a harlot
A man is reduced to a crust of bread;
And an adulteress will prey upon his precious life.
Can a man take fire to his bosom,
And his clothes not be burned?
Can one walk on hot coals,
And his feet not be seared?
So is he who goes in to his neighbor's wife;
Whoever touches her shall not be innocent.
People do not despise a thief
If he steals to satisfy himself when he is starving.
Yet when he is found, he must restore sevenfold;
He may have to give up all the substance of his house.
Whoever commits adultery with a woman
lacks understanding;
He who does so destroys his own soul.
Wounds and dishonor he will get,
And his reproach will not be wiped away.
For jealousy is a husband's fury;
Therefore he will not spare in the day of vengeance.
He will accept no recompense,
Nor will he be appeased though you give many gifts.
Proverbs 6:23-35 NKJ

My son, keep my words,
And treasure my commands within you.
Keep my commands and live,
And my law as the apple of your eye.
Bind them on your fingers;
Write them on the tablet of your heart.
Say to wisdom, "You [are] my sister,"
And call understanding [your] nearest kin,
That they may keep you from the immoral woman,
From the seductress [who] flatters with her words.
For at the window of my house
I looked through my lattice,
And saw among the simple,
I perceived among the youths,
A young man devoid of understanding,
Passing along the street near her corner;
And he took the path to her house
In the twilight, in the evening,
In the black and dark night.
And there a woman met him,
With the attire of a harlot, and a crafty heart.
She was loud and rebellious,
Her feet would not stay at home.
At times she was outside, at times in the open square,
Lurking at every corner.
So she caught him and kissed him;
With an impudent face she said to him:
"I have peace offerings with me;
Today I have paid my vows.
So I came out to meet you,
Diligently to seek your face,
And I have found you.
I have spread my bed with tapestry,

For my husband is not at home;
He has gone on a long journey;
He has taken a bag of money with him,
And will come home on the appointed day."
With her enticing speech she caused him to yield,
With her flattering lips she seduced him.
Immediately he went after her, as an ox goes
to the slaughter,
Or as a fool to the correction of the stocks,
Till an arrow struck his liver.
As a bird hastens to the snare,
He did not know it would cost his life.
Now therefore, listen to me, my children;
Pay attention to the words of my mouth:
Do not let your heart turn aside to her ways,
Do not stray into her paths;
For she has cast down many wounded,
And all who were slain by her were strong men.
Her house is the way to hell,
Descending to the chambers of death.

Proverbs 7:1-27 NKJ

Contents

Foreword

When the Lord sent Neil and Noline our way, they were crushed and devastated. They had been told that God would never allow them to minister again, that He had written *Ichabod* over their lives. Every day we tried to assure them that this was simply not true, but they were so wounded that six months passed before we saw the first glimmer of hope in their eyes.

Today, as we watch this tremendously anointed couple minister to the lives of others, we wonder what would have become of them had no one loved them enough to disciple them to healing. And we wonder how many thousands of other fallen leaders are living with the lie that God is through with them. Someone must reach them with the truth of God's grace and His restoration power!

Being anointed is not the question. The Scriptures declare: *"For the gifts and the calling of God are irrevocable"* (Romans 11:29 NKJ). God anoints His vessels for the good of those *receiving* the ministry, not to prove the worthiness of the minister. If an anointing were only present in the absence of sin, then any sin of any type would stop the anointing in a minister's life. Any minister who has ever had an argument on the way to the pulpit can be thankful this is not the case. The presence of the anointing simply indicates that God desires to minister to others through the vessel of His choice.

The key issue is not can God forgive adultery and restore men and women to the ministry. The key issue is how can we develop godly character in the hearts and lives of servants of God that will keep them from falling again and again in the future. Neil Rhodes is an excellent example of a leader who continued in secret sin for years, thinking that because he could still minister with great anointing, his sin was not hindering his ministry. No doubt many people were blessed by the Lord through him during those years. Unfortunately, the cancer of sin continued its work within Neil's own heart and soul, eventually poisoning everyone around him.

Leaders who have fallen into sin do not need condemnation or modern-day tar and feathering. They need loving discipline that will retrain and reshape areas of character deficiency in their lives. For this to happen, though, the leader must become totally honest and humble regarding these issues, coming out from the hiding place that the anointing has provided.

This is often difficult to do when he or she is fighting for survival in marriage and family. The sin strikes the first blow to relationship, but when the entire family is "thrown to the wolves" as part of the "disciplinary" process, few marriages can endure the ravages that follow. Many leaders are forced to seek secular employment for which they are unskilled and untrained. This often leads to minimum-wage jobs which, in turn, leads to financial crises within the home. Often the couple is left to seek their own counselors, and many end up seeing no one because of the added expense. It is not long before the already-weakened relationship begins to crumble under the added pressures. This, coupled with the belief that they have failed not only mankind but God Himself, is enough to bring even the heartiest relationships to an end.

We are convinced that the key to restoring fallen leadership is loving discipline that calls them into account daily regarding old patterns and habits while loving them unconditionally, giving them hope and purpose. For a leader to submit to this discipline, there must be brokenness and a willingness to admit the need for character training. A simple remorse for having been caught in sin is not enough.

Neil and Noline are beautiful examples of lives torn apart by sin and deceit yet restored by the powerful love and discipline of Jesus Christ. We pray that their book will give hope and vision to the thousands of other leaders who sit by the wayside, believing God is through with them. If the Church is to triumph over sin in the lives of our leaders, we must begin to restore them and their families through systematic loving discipline that heals first the individual, then the couple, and then the family. Until *all* of these are healed, we have not completed the restoration.

God bless you and your family today!
Mike and Marilyn Phillipps

Introduction

We spent the first thirty years of our lives on the beautiful continent of Africa. The country of our birth, Rhodesia, now called Zimbabwe, is situated in south-central Africa. Because we were born to British immigrants, and grew up in a British colony, our lives were naturally shaped by British traditions. Strict discipline was the order of the day, and we wore uniforms to schools that were, for the most part, not coeducational. Consequently, although Noline and I lived just a mile from each other, we went to school on opposite sides of town.

Life in the Africa of our youth was not hectic. In fact, when we were not changing governments, it was a very relaxed place to grow up — maybe too relaxed. The easy pace and the fact that our schools only ran half a day left plenty of time for us to get into trouble — which I did on a regular basis as a youth.

I cannot blame Rhodesian society for how I turned out, but it definitely played a major role in the early formation of my character. Patterns forged in those early years greatly affected my behavior throughout my teenage years and on into my marriage. I seemed to make the same mistakes over and over again and most of my lessons were learned the hard way, often accompanied by many unnecessary hurts and bruises. Ultimately, my marriage suffered the most from these patterns created by the sins of my youth; for, although I had become a Christian, I fell into adultery. The ramifications of my failures were so far-reaching that I feel compelled to warn others who may be facing similar pitfalls.

My sin of adultery brought our marriage to the breaking point, as Noline seriously considered divorcing me; and, of course, adultery put in danger my relationship to God. Adultery is everything that He is not. It is committed in secret and lies kept in secret, while God is light and hides nothing in darkness. Adultery is conceived in lust, the very opposite of God, who is Love. Adultery is, therefore, damaging to covenant relationships, our relationship to the Lord and to our spouses. The Lord warns us consistently in His Word not to entangle ourselves in the destructive force of adultery, and shows us that those who commit this sin do so to their own hurt.

My sin was all the more serious due to the fact that I was an ordained minister of the Gospel and the pastor of a church. I, of all people, should have known better. Fortunately, God intervened in our case, brought us to a place of repentance, to the arms

willing to nurture us to healing and who patiently instructed us in the building of godly character; and He brought us to a new home in the United States. We are grateful to Him for thus introducing hope, a precious commodity, into our desperate situation. Our prayer is that this book will become an instrument of God's love to many other hurting couples and will minister hope to them.

Of equal importance, we would like this book to be a caution to those in full-time ministry, especially the pastorate, to not let their work replace their relationship with their wives and to not allow themselves to be fooled into thinking that adultery is somehow acceptable or justifiable. It isn't. The principles shared in this book apply to people in other professions, as well, including the workaholics in commerce and industry and the white- or blue-collar workers who love the work place more than their own home.

Noline and I write from a unique perspective. We understand firsthand the pitfalls and the traps the enemy has set to ensnare married couples today. We understand what it's like to feel that your marriage is doomed, to feel that everything is lost and there is no love left between you. We have been there.

Jesus rescued our relationship and infused His love, His life, and His peace into our lives and marriage. With His resurrection power, He restored to us a "one-flesh union" which we thoroughly enjoy

us a "one-flesh union" which we thoroughly enjoy today. Furthermore, we are convinced that God can and will do the same for you, whoever you are, and whatever your circumstances happen to be.

The reasons our modern society is experiencing more marital problems today than ever before are apparent to all, but the solutions are not nearly as obvious. We live in an age when life is traveling at the speed of a runaway freight train. The "quick fix" mentality pervades our society and greatly influences the Body of Christ. We all want easy solutions to our problems, but what we desperately need is a lasting word from God. We need His revelation for all of life's problems. The quick fix never lasts, but the principles of the Lord stand for all eternity. Our wholehearted prayer is that God will quicken His truth to your hearts by His Holy Spirit as you read this book. We want you to learn and profit from the mistakes we made, and may the fullness of the Lord's plan for you be manifest in every aspect of your life as you reach out for the vision of *Refilling the Jars.*

Neil Rhodes
Denver, Colorado

Chapter 1

Dismissal

Flee from sexual immorality. All other sins a man commits are outside his body, but he who sins sexually sins against his own body.

1 Corinthians 6:18 NIV

NEIL:

The Sunday morning after I confessed my sin of adultery to my wife, it was my turn to preach. For the first time in five years, I took a deep breath and truthfully declared from the pulpit, "There is absolutely *nothing* between my wife and me. We are *totally transparent* with each other."

Everyone in the congregation responded with a resounding "Amen!" Everyone, that is, except the "other woman." She sat staring at me from her pew with an incredulous look on her face, betraying any attempt to hide what she was thinking. "I don't believe what I'm hearing!" her eyes screamed at me.

Rapidly her initial surprise had given way to unbelief and then was replaced by a stony glare. I could only imagine the thoughts that raced through her heart and mind at that moment. *Did he actually tell his wife? How could he be so stupid?*

It was amazing that our sordid little secret had been kept for five long years. It had come to light in one moment of brokenhearted confession to my wife. I couldn't bear the pain and the shame any longer. Yet now I faced a new grief as I wondered what lay ahead with the other woman's reaction.

I didn't have long to wait for the unavoidable confrontation. The service had barely ended when she cornered me in the foyer and, at point blank range, demanded, "Did you tell Noline about us?"

"Yes," I replied.

"Did you tell her everything?

"Yup!"

Forces Set In Motion

That simple dialogue did two things that changed my life forever: First, it destroyed the soul-ties forged in sin that had bound us together for five years as joint possessors of a sad secret and a heavy chain of guilt and sorrow. Secondly, it ended my pastoral career. My former lover went immediately to the senior pastor's wife with a moral accusation against me; and the pastor's wife, in turn, relayed the accusation to her husband, who immediately called the elders to set up an emergency meeting. As a result of this meeting, I was dismissed from my position with the church and ordered to make a public confession.

The saints gathered the following Sunday as usual, unaware that they were about to witness what I believed to be an execution at the church gallows. That morning the senior pastor preached one of the heaviest sermons I had ever heard; but, strangely, I felt detached from the whole ordeal, as though it were happening to someone else. I don't know if this was God's way of protecting me, or if the humiliation of it all just anesthetized me. I was there physically, but the reality of it all didn't hit me at the time. Later that evening I would feel the full weight of the penalty I was to pay for my rebellious, deceitful, and immoral past.

I had been instructed to stand before the congregation and confess to an "immoral indiscretion" with an "anonymous person." I was not to identify the woman because she was sitting in the congregation, and the senior pastor and elders did not want to embarrass her.

As the time approached, the more I thought about these restrictions placed on me by the leadership of the church, the more I struggled with them. My mind raced wildly with the possibilities of what people might think if I told them only that much. I had been serving as pastor over the Christian school. What if the people thought that my unidentified "indiscretion" involved a child? They might come to the conclusion that I was a child molester! I couldn't take that chance, so I made up my mind to avoid that possibility and to try to salvage my image at any cost.

When I stood before the congregation in that morning service, therefore, I knowingly told a "partial truth." Disregarding the explicit instructions of the pastor and elders, I told the people that I had something to confess, that I had been guilty of giving "someone" an "ungodly hug." In reality, I *had* recently given my former lover a hug in her apartment. She had resisted any further advances, so the matter had stopped there; but I thought "an ungodly hug" would sound a lot better than the truth. So even my "confession" was given in such a way as to hold up the wall of deception that concealed the real me from the people. I desperately hoped that no one would discover the truth.

My Deception Fails This Time

Things seemed to go well that morning, and I felt that I had succeeded. After all, I had managed to keep most of my professional image intact. When the congregation heard that we were being released from our pastoral duties, and all because of an "ungodly hug," many of them came to our defense. How unfair! Hadn't most everyone done similar things? My flesh gloried in the moment! The honest-but-flawed-human-being approach had apparently saved my reputation.

Had I accurately portrayed the incident? Yes and no. What I said was true, but it wasn't the whole truth. I had simply left out the little matter of my acts of adultery in the past and the five years I had spent justifying and hiding my sin. I thought I could get away with the sin and the cover up, but Jesus set a higher standard:

> *You have heard that it was said to those of old, 'You shall not commit adultery.' But I say to you that whoever looks at a woman to lust for her has already committed adultery with her in his heart.*
>
> Matthew 5:27-28

I still had sin in my heart at the time of the hug and would probably have gone to bed with the woman again (five years after our affair had ended) if she had not resisted my advances that day.

I was wrong to disregard the senior pastor's instructions. I should have confessed what a dirty dog I had really been. I was not only guilty of adultery, but also of the continual sin of self-justification. Yet I could not bring myself to accept the full consequences of my failure and, as a result, I was unable to repent and seek the forgiveness I desperately needed. Self-deception and my uncanny ability to quickly put on the right masks kept me from being one hundred percent real with the Word of God. I would need the help of others to recognize this blind spot in my life.

Consumed by my obsession to hide my secret failures and sin at any cost, I took offense with the senior pastor and the elders, and continued to justify myself, while directing my anger at them. It was a defense reaction to keep my flesh from being hurt. I don't know who said it first, but there is a great saying that describes my destiny and my folly: "God does not want to hurt our pride. He wants to kill it." My flesh was struggling to stay alive, and God was telling me to crucify it, once and for all.

My Ministry Ends

The pastor and elders were so upset with the direction that Sunday morning meeting had taken that they wrote letters and made phone calls to the whole congregation calling for another special meeting on the following Wednesday night. I was again required to come before the people, but this time for the *coup de grace*. I was firmly instructed to tell the congregation that I had lied and needed forgiveness. If that weren't enough, the leadership further informed me that because of my lack of cooperation in the matter, they were now forced to reveal the truth about my past. Thus, my wall of deceit and concealment fell in ruins around me. The people who had supported me in sympathy now saw me for what I really was — a liar and an adulterer. I was uncovered, laid bare, and demolished.

I didn't know it at the time, but this was the beginning of a process of restoration that was described by the prophet Jeremiah:

See, I have this day set you over the nations and over the kingdoms, To root out and to pull down, To destroy and to throw down, To build and to plant. Jeremiah 1:10

The rooting and the tearing down were now accomplished, and the Lord could begin a major cleanup of His broken and defiled vessel. Only then could the process of rebuilding and replanting take place. I had been dismissed, now I needed to be restored.

Chapter 2

A Rebel Is Saved

*The thief comes only to steal and kill and destroy;
I have come that they may have life, and have it to
the full.* John 10:10 NIV

NEIL:

Toward the end of my senior year in high school
I had a confrontation with a teacher that was to ad-
versely affect my future. I can still hear my blus-
tery words, "If that gay touches my butt, I'm going
to take a swing at him!" The man's well-earned reputation for touching boys where he had no business
touching them left no doubt in any of our minds that
he was a homosexual. My feisty rhetoric was soon
put to the test when the teacher tried to touch me in
shop class. My classmates were watching to see my
reaction. When the time came, everything happened
so fast that I didn't have time to think. Instinct took
over and, in total disgust and revulsion, I picked up
a short 2x4 and swung it at his head.

Although I somehow stopped the board inches from the face of my abuser, that incident put an end to my formal schooling. I was taken to the principal's office and severely disciplined, with no opportunity to justify my actions, so I had enough of school. To my parents, I was just a part of the '60s rebellion, so they didn't force me to go back and finish the year. Their attitude was, "You've made your bed, now lie in it!"

Things quickly went downhill from there.

A Close Call

"Watch out!" Nick yelled.

I shouted back, "I can't stop this stupid thing!" Seconds later, Nick jumped off the bike and rolled down the embankment. I had just enough time to see him flying over the rocks before I looked ahead toward the on-ramp of the interstate.

Traffic was heavy, and the brakes on my motor bike were not working the way they should. I was hurtling headlong into the path of a semi-tractor trailer going seventy miles an hour. I turned the bike to face the semi and somehow managed to let it pass my front wheel with only inches to spare before I entered sideways into traffic. I got through both lanes by the skin of my teeth and then began to maneuver the bike across the median and into the next set of lanes. Glancing at the traffic, I determined it was clear enough for a direct crossing to the other side of the road. *I've made it!* I thought.

Then, WHAM!

Time seemed to stop in mid air.

I've been hit, I thought, as I flew through the air. *Why don't I feel any pain?* THUD! CRUNCH! I hit the ground. I could hear my bike being dragged down the road with sounds of metal scraping on blacktop. The squealing of melting tires added to the orchestra of chaos. Then I heard only silence, a deafening silence that seemed to last for an eternity.

Gradually the hum of rush-hour traffic drifted through to me, slowly bringing everything back to normal. With great effort, I stood up, with one foot on the grassy shoulder and the other on the blacktop. I was bleeding profusely from three different facial wounds, and my left eye was filled with blood, blocking my vision. My left hand and wrist were hanging limp.

I tried to move my hand, but it wouldn't move. The bone of my left thumb was protruding through the skin on the palm of my hand. There was a bloody gash on my side, and my left pant leg was torn and blood-soaked. Strangely, I couldn't feel a thing. Later, when the effects of the LSD finally wore off at the hospital, the pain was excruciating.

Drugs and marijuana had become a major part of my daily life for most of the two years since I had dropped out of school. My older brother had invited me to go to South Africa. There he had led the way, introducing me to a life-style that was supposed to be a "statement of peace" to the chaotic world we blamed our parents for creating.

My friend Nick and I had been tripping on LSD at the time of the accident. We were convinced we could fly, so Nick had decided to balance himself while standing on the seat of the motorcycle. I was standing on the footrests while I let the handle bars go free, my arms outstretched to the wind to "help us fly better." We were absolutely convinced that we would leave the ground at any second — that is until Nick noticed, in horror, that the crowded interstate was just thirty yards below us. We were moving along at about thirty miles an hour when we crested the hill, but, since we were so high on drugs, it seemed like we were just crawling along. We felt like we could just get off and walk, if we wanted to.

A Mercedes Benz had been concealed behind a truck at the exact time I glanced back at the oncoming traffic. Moving at a high rate of speed, the luxury car had pulled into the passing lane as I cleared the first of the two lanes. It was this car that hit me, the full force of the impact hitting the rear of the motorcycle. A split second's difference would have brought the full impact directly upon me, and there is no way I could have lived through that. God had clearly intervened on my behalf.

I spent the next agonizing days in the hospital,

but those few days seemed like an eternity, and I would long remember them. When I was finally released, I had eighteen stitches in my face and side, my left arm was encased in plaster. I had not been in good health even before the crash. Continuous rounds of barbiturates had stripped my weight down to 130 pounds, and my 6′ 2″ frame was nothing but skin and bones.

I had imagined that life as a hippie would be 'cool,' but I had learned, the hard way, that being 'cool' has its downside. My life had deteriorated to the point that I was sleeping on the roofs of apartment complexes or curling up in the back stairways of inner-city buildings to get some much-needed rest. I was shocked by this turn of events, and in desperate loneliness I had cried out only three days earlier, "Oh, God, just come and take my life!" Little did I realize how seriously God took that prayer.

Looking back now, I have no doubt that the Lord used all of the difficult circumstances, including the cold rooftops and the painful hours confined to a hospital bed, to draw me back to Himself. I now found myself boarding a train for home.

The Natural Wine of Young Love

As soon as I reached the familiar streets of my hometown, the first thing I wanted to do was look up Noline Wakefield. We had known each other since we were twelve, and she was very special to me.

I will never forget the circumstances of our meeting: One summer a friend across the road asked me to go camping with a group of friends. I said, "Great!" Privately I wondered why I had to pay so much money to go camping. Little did I realize that I had just bought myself a full week at a Baptist youth camp. (It was a good thing he hadn't told me the whole truth. There was no way I would have gone to a *church*-related activity — especially one I had to pay for!)

The minute I arrived at the camp, I knew I had made a big mistake. Thanks to my "friend" I was now stuck in this dreadful place with some very weird people who were always singing and going to one church meeting after another. I managed to avoid the meetings that week, but I did get something out of my time there that was more than worthwhile. I met a very interesting and friendly girl. She was older than me, but when the time came for parting, she offered to introduce me to her sister who was my age. I thought to myself, *This was not such a bad week after all!*

A week later, I paid my friend and her family a visit, and her sister was alright —although she chased me around the dining room table with magic markers. She seemed to be a little immature for twelve, but she was a lot of fun. I thought Noline Wakefield was pretty and made up my mind that I would like to see her again. The feeling was mutual.

After that first meeting, in fact, Noline and I became childhood sweethearts.

The time we had spent together over the coming years had been like something out of a story book. We did things as a team, whether it was cleaning rabbit cages or some summer job. The only downside to our childhood romance was that Noline's parents did not approve of it because I was not a Christian; but we didn't let that stop us. From very early we felt we were destined to be together — with or without her parents' permission. We had a lot of *natural wine* between us and were intoxicated with each other's love. The Song of Solomon seemed to be written especially for us:

> *You have stolen my heart, my sister, my bride; you have stolen my heart with one glance of your eyes, with one jewel of your necklace. How delightful is your love, my sister, my bride! How much more pleasing is your love than wine, and the fragrance of your perfume than any spice!*
> *Like an apple tree among the trees of the forest is my lover among the young men. I delight to sit in his shade, and his fruit is sweet to my taste. He has taken me to the banquet hall, and his banner over me is love.*
> Song of Solomon 4:9-10, 3:3-4 NIV

As we look back on those days, we know — beyond a shadow of a doubt — that the deep friendship we developed early on was the only thing that held us together later in life and enabled us to survive the storms that lay ahead.

Despite my love for Noline, my growing up years were far from idyllic. Early in life I had noticed that the boys who seemed to have the most fun were the party-goers, and I decided to run with them rather than concentrate on school work. Thus, from a very early age, I ran with the wrong crowd. Fornication was rampant among these friends. They knew who was "easy"; and since I had a serious lack of discipline in my life, I didn't have the fortitude to resist such open and available temptation. I thus became entangled in immorality at a young age, despite the strong feelings I had for Noline, who was just the opposite.

From a strong Christian background, Noline had given her heart to the Lord at the age of five and had grown up in a godly home where the Bible was the standard of right and wrong. Her motives and way of life were virtuous and pure. She had received loving discipline in her childhood, something that was absent from our home. She firmly said NO to areas of personal compromise and, though it aggravated me, I highly respected her for it. Unfortunately, I didn't have the resolve to keep myself pure for her and indulged myself with other girls from time to time.

A Rebel Is Saved

Noline was completely different from those other girls, and I knew in my heart that she was the girl I wanted to marry. More than anything else in life, it seemed, I wanted to have this pure virgin as my wife forever. At the ripe old age of fifteen, we asked Noline's mother if we could get married. That was a serious mistake.

Noline's mother wanted nothing to do with me and she warned Noline to avoid me at all costs. Every time their family would pass our house in their car, she would say, "Noline, Watch out for those boys!" Noline obeyed — by carefully "watching" for me so she could wave and blow me a secret kiss. We were in love and continually dreamed of our future together.

We remained sweethearts through my high school years, even when I secretly dated other girls. Noline was good for me. She loved me for who I was, not for who I pretended to be in front of my peers. When I wanted to be appreciated, I visited Noline. When I wanted to party and be wild, I ran with my other friends.

When I had made that fateful move to South Africa, I had asked Noline to accompany me. She had refused, wanting to finish her education. This, and my failure to write her from South Africa, lead to a definite cooling of our relationship, and we both began to date other people.

Still, Noline was the first person I wanted to see when I got off that train, and I set about to see if I could find her. I soon discovered that she was now in college and had her own car; and, when I saw her, she looked as beautiful as ever. Her reaction to seeing me again was difficult to figure out at first. First, there was a hint of shock in her facial expression, but then my appearance *was* rather shocking. I had completely changed. I was no longer the same "boy down the road" she had grown up with.

There was a certain awkwardness to our meeting because we were worlds apart in thinking and living, but, despite my shocking appearance and the awkwardness of the moment, I could sense that Noline was happy to see me. If I had ever doubted it, I knew that day that I really did love her and wanted to spend the rest of my life with her.

Saved!

The next weekend Noline and her sister tried to get me to go to church. "No, I am not going to church," I answered. "I don't need church. All I need is a joint." Despite my lack of cooperation, Noline sat quietly, as her newly-married sister and brother-in-law witnessed to me about Christ's love for sinners.

When I learned that Noline had been planning to visit her sister, who lived a hundred miles away, I had started scheming to accompany her. "Interested in having someone ride with you?" I asked.

"Sure," Noline answered.

And that is how I landed on that couch for the personal sermon I was enduring. That simple visit had turned into a "Holy War" between the Christians and the infidel. Finally I put my foot down and declared I was not going to the meeting, and they relented.

Well, that's the morning service out of the way, I thought triumphantly. Her sister and brother-in-law went on to church and Noline and I, at last, had some quiet time together to catch up on old times and discuss our friends.

When the others returned from church, however, the Holy War resumed. "Please, won't you come to the evening service? Please?" they were asking again.

Persistent people! I mused.

"Okay!" I finally gave in, just to get them off my back. Although I had been baptized as a baby in a Methodist church, I had grown up unchurched. I had gone to church a few times in my life, and it hadn't seemed all that bad, so I agreed to go with them. No one warned me that I had made a deal to spend two hours in the same room with a fanatical, Bible-preaching, hand-clapping, vibrant community of believers.

I sat at the back of the place feeling conspicuous and totally out of place. I was the only person in the building wearing ripped-up jeans, T-shirt, and sandals. My long, greasy hair, the stitches in my face, and the plaster cast on my arm only confirmed that I did not fit in with this crowd.

Throughout the sermon, the preacher did not take his eyes off me, and it made me feel very uncomfortable. It seemed like he was directing his whole sermon at me. Occasionally I shifted my head to the side to look out the window for a few moments, but every time I looked back, he was still staring right at me. I felt strangely drawn to what the man was saying, but was sure I could listen better if he would quit that staring business.

At the end of the sermon, the preacher invited all those who wanted to "get right with God" to go to the front. Suddenly, I stood to my feet and started walking to the front, all the time thinking to myself, *What am I doing? Neil, you're crazy!*

A voice was screaming inside of me, *"You're not going to kneel down and pray like an idiot, are you?"* My brain was condemning me, but once I got to my knees, I poured my heart out to Jesus of Nazareth. That night in, January of 1972, I received Jesus Christ as my Lord and Savior. The shackles of sin fell off, and I became a new creation in Him. I was born-again, baptized, and delivered from drugs in a few moments of repentance and confession. I was filled with the Holy Spirit and sensed the empowerment of new life surging through me. My sins were gone, washed away, and I had new life in the Lord. A rebel had been saved.

Chapter 3

Living On the Sand, Before the Storm

For where your treasure is, there your heart will be also ... . But everyone who hears these sayings of Mine, and does not do them, will be like a foolish man who built his house on the sand: and the rain descended, the floods came, and the winds blew and beat on that house; and it fell. And great was its fall. Matthew 6:21, 7:26-27 NKJ

NOLINE:

When Neil gave his heart to Christ, I thought my parents would finally accept him and give their blessing to our relationship, so I wasn't prepared for their reaction. They were still skeptical about Neil; and, with every passing day, my fear of losing the man I loved to another woman kept growing. This was heightened when Neil was drafted into the Army to fight in the Rhodesian Civil War. The thought of him dying in battle, having never con-summated our love, was sometimes more than I could bear at times. I just couldn't accept the possibility of going through life without Neil.

I dreaded the day that he would leave for basic training, and when that day finally came, we spent the entire day and evening together, talking and looking into each other's eyes, wondering if we would ever see one another again. How could we say good-bye? It seemed impossible.

It was a heart-rending, bittersweet day of para-lyzed fear — and uncontrollable love; for in our heightened emotion, we did what I never intended for us to do before marriage. We willingly aban-doned ourselves to each other in sexual intimacy.

I have never blamed Neil for what happened that night, for I wanted him as much as he wanted me. It was a mutual decision, and a wrong one that was to have lasting consequences.

I had always intended to wait until our wedding night, and I wish we had waited, but, at that mo-ment, all I could think about was keeping Neil close to me. My actions that night were not justified "just because I loved him," and my emotional attachment didn't add an ounce of legitimacy to our decision to sleep together. What we did was wrong, and it took me many years to finally forgive myself in Christ and change my self-image as a failure. It would be many years later before I was finally delivered from the spirit of fear that began influencing my life that first night and continued for many years afterward.

NEIL:

Flee Youthful Lusts

It is no wonder God's Word warns us to *"flee from sexual immorality"* (1 Corinthians 6:18). The human sex drive is a God-given passion. We were never meant to fight it. We are to flee from it until we are married. It is only in the context of marriage that a sexual relationship can be safely nurtured and cultivated.

Noline and I were in love, but lust and impatience had taken control of our hearts and emotions and we had awakened the sleeping giant of sexual passion.

I have always blamed myself for what happened that night. Noline had always kept herself pure in this regard. Thinking now of being away from her for long periods, I pressed her for intimacy, and it was easier for her to submit that night than to resist.

Things were never the same after that. We slept together that night, and, in the morning, Noline drove me to the barracks to report for basic training; but, by our actions, we had loosed a passion neither of us were able to control.

We continued to meet each other every time I could get my hands on a weekend pass, and there was no way we could go back to just holding hands. It seemed impossible to turn back. We loved each other so passionately that, despite our best intentions to control ourselves, we ended up yielding to each other on every visit.

When Noline told me over the phone that she was pregnant, I was elated with the idea of being a father, but I was more relieved than anything else, relieved that, at last, we would have an excuse to get married. The news was not as well received by our parents, especially hers. They were greatly disappointed in their daughter. From that day on, however, we felt justified in sleeping together. After all, we told ourselves, "God sees us as already married, even if our parents don't."

Almost one year to the day after I had given my life to Christ, we entered into a marriage covenant, the most sacred of all human relationships, with a new family member already on the way. Could we make it as man and wife and as responsible parents? Time would tell.

I thought I was ready to be married and ready to be a father, but, looking back, I'm sure that I was not ready for either responsibility. In later years, I would wonder time and again what had caused me to fail; for I had indeed failed God, failed my wife, failed my children, failed my family and failed my congregation.

Several things stand out to me about my early years of life that have made me believe that if I had received proper mentoring, proper disciplining, proper instruction in godly living, early enough, perhaps I could have avoided my downfall. At the very least, they are worthy of mention.

As I later looked back on my life and tried to analyze it I recognized in myself rebellion, selfishness, longing for approval, and a driving need to succeed, all factors that may have, in some way or other, contributed to my sin.

Discipline was one of the biggest areas of failure in my life. I not only lacked self-discipline, but I resented anyone else who tried to discipline me. I repented of this failure over and over again. I somehow feel that it was this lack of discipline and hatred of authority figures that allowed me to eventually open the door to something that God despises in a man — rebellion.

As a young child, I never really knew the security and reassurance provided by the restraints of biblical parental discipline. Screaming and yelling seemed to be the favorite form of "discipline" in our home. By the time I turned fifteen, I already knew the answer when I asked to take my mother's car to a party. "No!" My response to that answer was to sneak out of the house, push the car down the driveway and onto the road, "hot-wire" the ignition and cruise off to be with my friends.

My dad caught me in this late one night as I brought the car to a silent halt in the driveway. He had heard me earlier and had waited for me. His method of dealing with the situation, true to form, was ranting and raving, but that was the end of it. There was no discipline applied and no consequences for my actions — just yelling.

Another time I nearly overdosed on barbiturates at school. I became nauseous, disoriented, lost all the color in my face, and began to tremble. I was taken to the school nurse, followed by a prompt visit from the principal. One look at my pupils told him the whole story (they were no larger than the tip of a pin). The principal called my father and asked him to take me home. When he picked me up, my father asked me if I had taken any drugs. I told him no, and that was the end of the confrontation. At that point, he seemed to have no desire to rein me in, and this lack of parental constraint in my life did nothing but encourage a continued life of rebellion. Since I always seemed to be able to "get away with murder" at home with no consequences, I entered my adult life with the belief that I could do most anything I wanted and get away with it.

Because of my lack of discipline, I was unable to resist when doors of temptation opened to me.

But each one is tempted when, by his own evil

desire, he is dragged away and enticed. Then, af-
ter desire has conceived, it gives birth to sin; and
sin, when it is full-grown, gives birth to death.

James 1:14-15 NIV

At a very young age I began to operate out of deception, with my list of lies and fabrications constantly growing. But deception is very tricky. As you weave your lies to deceive others, the disease infects your heart and head, leading you to actually believe that what you are doing is okay. The Bible says:

... evil men and impostors will go from bad to
worse, deceiving and being deceived.

2 Timothy 3:13 NIV

I began to tell myself, *Hey, I'm not really doing anything wrong. This is just how life is.*

I am now convinced that Christian character is formed in children through consistent, loving discipline in spiritual matters, by teaching them to pray and read the Bible, and by attending Sunday school on a regular basis. It is Christian character that forms the strong fiber that carries us through the tough days in life. People without character will always see the most precious things in life slip through their fingers.

A lady once called a talk show host to ask where

she could find a company "to get the best consolidation loan" so that she could continue her runaway credit card spending. That woman didn't need to resolve her debt problem, she needed to correct the lack of discipline in her spending habits. In other words, she needed to live within her means by cutting back her expenditures to match her income, even if it hurt. If all she did was consolidate her debt into one loan, a year later she would have her consolidation loan plus another twelve months of new credit card debt to pay off!

I was in the same situation as the credit card queen, only my problem was moral, not financial. Every time I made a wrong moral decision, I wanted forgiveness for my wrongdoing, but the real problem was much deeper and more serious than the wrongs I was committing. I didn't have the Christian character that can only be developed by strong, loving discipline and clear-cut guidelines.

My new life in Christ brought Noline and me closer than we had ever been before, but I lacked the character to develop the relationship in a godly way. Noline had remained true to herself and to the Lord during my wild years of drugs and fornication and it was these qualities that greatly attracted me to her. The fact that she had always refused my sexual advances during our dating phase did not diminish my appreciation of her. In fact, it only enhanced her attractiveness in my eyes.

Living On the Sand, Before the Storm

Then, when I was drafted into the military, our romance seemed to deepen even more with each new day. I knew, beyond a shadow of a doubt, that she was the girl I wanted to marry; and, besides, we were both Christians now. Surely that counted for something. The end result of my theorizing, however, led to much hurt and to our losing the respect of our family and peers for a long period of time.

Some might say that our premarital relationship was inevitable. I have heard it said that if you spend three hundred hours with a person of the opposite sex, you will either break up or be intimate with one another. We were spending more and more time with each other, and being more and more intimate with each passing day.

During my life of sin, I had honed my talent of pressuring girls to yield themselves to me sexually, and when I applied these skills to getting Noline into bed before leaving for my boot camp training, I didn't think of it as manipulating her — since I was sure she now wanted me as much as I wanted her. What I didn't realize was that I was displeasing God and setting a very dangerous precedent for my future life. I was living on the sand, before the storm.

Chapter 4

Storm Clouds Gather

Lord, when You went out from Seir, when You marched from the field of Edom, the earth trembled and the heavens poured, the clouds also poured water; the mountains gushed before the Lord, this Sinai, before the Lord God of Israel.

Judges 5:4-5

NEIL:

January 13, 1973, our wedding day! We were delighted, excited, and definitely relieved to be free of the intense pressure of living in sin. Our childhood dreams had become a reality. We were finally husband and wife! Now we could freely drink deep of the "wine" or our passionate love for each other, without guilt. Our intoxication with each other seemed to be unending, and our lives and our marriage seemed to be wonderful.

We spent our honeymoon at a little cottage located fifteen miles outside of town. For four unforgettable days we enjoyed swimming, eating, and making love. The remaining six days of my ten-day military pass were spent establishing a new home together. I only had a few months of military service left, and we began to make plans for the future. Life was not as easy as we had imagined, and we didn't have long to wait for our first serious disagreement.

The First Confrontations

"What?" exclaimed Noline. "You want us to get up, get dressed in our Sunday best, and go to church the day after our wedding?" My reasoning was perfectly logical to me. Just as I had lived for the world, so now I would live for God — even if it meant "showing myself faithful" at the expense of my wife's feelings the day after our wedding. Some of my insistence may have also been motivated by my desire to obtain the approval of the people around us. We were starting a new life together, with each other, and with the Lord, and we wanted to start it right. So I insisted, got my way, and set off that morning with my new bride in tow, rushing to make it to church in time for the morning worship service. This incident could have been cause for alarm. Did I need to learn to learn to live out my Christianity without being religious.

In the years to come, I believe, I sometimes created a religious camouflage to keep others from seeing what was really going on in my heart. I felt I had to look good for others and feared that if people knew the real me, they would not accept me. Part of this was due to seeds of rejection sowed in my child-hood.

The Seeds of Rejection and the Resulting Branches

My parents were excellent providers for us, even in hard times. As children, we never felt the pinch of hard times, because they absorbed the sacrifice. When it came to being involved in my life, however, they just were not there, and this sowed a seed that was to germinate later in life.

My parents never openly rejected me, quite the contrary; but they did not provide the caring father-ing or mothering I needed. They both worked "8-5" jobs and were seldom home. Consequently, I grew up without boundaries, coming and going as I pleased.

There were other aspects of rejection that I felt. I remember exactly my feelings when, at the age of six and in the first grade, I noticed that many of my friends got a kiss from their mother or father when they were dropped off at school. This sort of thing was not done in our household. There was almost no display of affection at all. Seeing the affection other children received touched me deeply, and I decided to get a kiss from my mom before leaving for school the next day.

Since I walked to school, my kiss would have to come at home. So the next morning after breakfast, I got up from the table, walked over to where my mom was sitting, and reached up to kiss her good-bye. That simple act made me the focus of family ridicule. Everyone in the family — my older brother, my two older sisters, and even my parents — laughed and teased me about "kissing Mommy." As young as I was, I still made an oath never to embarrass myself like that again, and I obviously never forgot the incident.

Rejection is like a taproot that reaches deep and affects nearly every area of life, like the root of which the Apostle Paul spoke, when he said: *"If the part of the dough offered as firstfruits is holy, then the whole batch is holy; if the root is holy, so are the branches"* (Romans 11:16 NIV). Years later, realizing that the reverse was also true, I began to identify the many branches that were feeding off this main root.

Branch 1: Compulsive justification and rationalization.
   I constantly justified myself — whether I was right or wrong — because I feared I would be rejected if I acknowledged that I had done something wrong.

Branch 2: Failing to say "No!" in areas of moral compromise. Once I gained someone's confidence, I could never seem to say no — even when the relationship wandered onto dangerously thin ice. I never took the way of escape the Lord provided because I was afraid of hurting the other person's feelings or of being rejected myself.

Branch 3: I had "itchy" feet. I always wanted to move on to better and greener pastures. Once I had established the foundation in a new area, I tended to move on. While I was still "new" to everyone, I could gain a great deal of acceptance from people; but I was secretly afraid that if I stayed a long time, my welcome would run out, and I would be rejected. I avoided facing my fear by arranging to move before anyone had a chance to reject me.

Branch 4: I was a slave to performance. Charts hung on my walls so I could keep track of everything going on in the ministry. I was a slave to those charts because performance governed my life. Nonperformance or poor performance were the fuel for rejection, so I felt that I simply had to perform to gain the acceptance of my overseers. I felt that if I worked really hard and did exceptionally well, those over me would be pleased, and I could somehow earn a place of respect among them.

These were not healthy attitudes and would, eventually, cause me to fall. These seeds, sown so deeply into my life, would one day spring up to challenge and nearly destroy our marriage. It was only after this root was dealt a death blow by the "double-edged sword" of the Word of God that we could be free in our marriage to grow without fear.

New Roles

For now, though, we were still the blissful newlyweds. Two of the greatest years of my life were 1972 and 1973. In 1972, my dramatic conversion and subsequent baptism in the Holy Spirit had cleansed away my sin and broken the devilish power of drugs over my life. The Holy Spirit had done the work, and I was ready to obey Him fully, for I was consumed with zeal for the Lord. And now, in 1973, we had, at last, been united in marriage.

When I got saved, no one had to tell me to take off the hippie garb and put on a suit. It was automatic. Unfortunately, I was just as eager to change Noline's life as I was to change my own, and I set about to do that — whether she liked it or not. I had her parade in front of me in each of her different dresses, and if I decided a dress was too short, it was put aside and never worn again. I also decided that her makeup had to go because it wasn't considered "spiritual" to look the way she did.

Years later, I had to repent for being such a chauvinistic male. I had exercised no consideration for what Noline felt and what she liked. I didn't ask her opinion about these things and never once considered that she might feel uncomfortable wearing the things *I* approved.

Shortly before we were married, Noline had made a fresh commitment to the Lord, was baptized in water and filled with the Holy Spirit. Now we were blessed to experience a time of revival for the whole church, especially the young people. The Lord had heard their cry and was moving in supernatural power to save them. Noline and I, therefore, were both "on fire" for the Lord in 1973 and that year, as husband and wife, both recognized God's call upon our lives.

I thought seriously about attending Bible college in Canada. Fortunately, however, there was enough interest among other students living in our area that our denomination established a national college of its own, and it just happened to be located in our home town. Since we were living in another town at the time, we made plans to move back home.

We could hardly wait for the day to arrive when we would pack up, put our furniture into storage, and head off to Bible college. Our little Debbie was born on August 27th that year, so we were excited to hear that arrangements had been made for baby-sitting services for the children of students of the Bible college.

In the fall of 1974, Noline and I attended our first classes and began our formal training for the ministry. We took three years of Bible college classes, and

try. We took three years of Bible college classes, and then were required to invest either two years on the mission field or in local church training before ordination. We fulfilled all the requirements over the next five years, and I was then ordained and set in as senior pastor of the church in our city.

Disappointment

I sometimes joke about how Bible college ruined our marriage, but there is more truth than humor in that statement. Although Bible college was the place where great vision and the call of God was developed in us, it was also the place where serious seeds of discontentment were planted deep within my soul. I saw our instructors as great role models, great examples for both of us to follow. The men were apt to teach, and they were powerful speakers in their own right. Some of them had experienced tremendous revival through their ministries at different times and seasons. They were all filled with wisdom and knowledge. I passionately patterned myself after those men, learning to speak like them, act like them, and even to walk like them.

But Noline simply refused to conform. All of the wives of the pastors who had influenced our lives could play the piano, lead ladies' meetings, and run the Sunday School Department, but not Noline. She not only didn't play the piano, she didn't even want to. I was sure this was a serious mistake and took it

the result was not pleasant. After a short and unhappy period of forced submission on her part, we all agreed it was in everyone's best interest to abandon the idea.

With piano playing out, I turned my efforts to "damage control" and to Noline mastering the techniques of leading the ladies' meetings. This didn't work either, however, since Noline is, by nature, introverted. She did not feel comfortable doing the ladies' meetings and, in the end, refused to continue to even try. In my mind, she now had two strikes against her.

Without knowing it, I had discovered one of Noline's greatest strengths — stubbornness. It is a powerful trait, when used for the right reasons. Noline digs in her heels when it comes to righteousness, reading the Word of God, tithes, prayer, and other spiritual matters. However, when it comes to doing something she doesn't want to do, forget it! No earthly power (or anxious husband) is going to budge her. This irritated me to no end, and, instead of realizing that I had discovered a strength, I had no appreciation for her stubbornness at all, considering it to be a hindrance to our ministry.

I encountered the same pattern when I tried to "help her" take charge of the Sunday School Department like any "normal" pastor's wife would. I finally had to admit there was no way Noline was going to take charge when there were so many other extroverts who could do it.

going to take charge when there were so many other extroverts who could do it.

This unwillingness, on the part of Noline, to take up the traditional role of the pastor's wife became one of the most controversial aspects of our marriage, one that drove me to distraction. Why was it that she — for who knows what reason — refused to fit the concept I envisioned for the ideal pastor's wife? And if she refused to be what she should be, how could I fulfill my own dreams of success?

The question was closed by the time we graduated from Bible school anyway because Noline had given birth to two more children in the meantime. To my utter dismay, at the time, she considered the children to be her primary ministry, preferring them over all of the traditional duties of the pastor's wife, duties that I considered very important. What could I do? I finally realized that I had no choice in the matter. I would just have to get used to it.

Because we could not agree on matters of ministry, and because ministry became my life, the "dynamic duo" began to drift further and further apart once we assumed the pastorate. If the truth were know, we were both too young and inexperienced to be pastoring; but, in my mind, I was persevering and pressing in to be a "mighty man of God," while Noline was doing nothing to help me be the perfect pastor. While she devoted her life to caring for the children, I judged and dismissed her efforts because, from my perspective, she had a serious lack of commitment and sense of duty to the ministry. I thus focused my frustration and criticism on her and rationalized away my own inabilities and personal shortcomings. This may sound familiar to other men in ministry.

This pattern of blaming others followed me throughout my pastoral ministry. When I was not blaming Noline, I blamed other people in our congregation. The only individual I didn't bless with my gift of criticism was myself. I just could never see when I was the one with the problem!

A New Approach

Since our relationship was no longer as happy and loving as we had hoped it would always be, Noline and I began to study the topics of marriage, relationships, and personalities. We wanted to know what was wrong with us. We each made a list and matched answer keys to find our personalities and "soul profiles," our spiritual gifts, and the temperaments behind our personalities. The process helped us some; but, for the most part, I was simply more aggravated at Noline for being an introvert in my extroverted ministry life.

The greatest irony of all this was that I still really loved Noline and was very attracted to her personality and temperament; but, when it came to ministry, I felt I needed someone who was completely the opposite of her. I wanted another me.

The bottom line of our problem, I am sure, was really my pride. I wanted Noline to make me look good. I expected her to complement my work in the ministry, and when she wouldn't (or couldn't) do it, I became frustrated. I began to entertain secret thoughts of admiration for other women who were talented in areas I thought Noline should have excelled in. "If only Noline were like so and so. If only she could play and sing like Jane, or lead Sunday School like Helen, we could have a great thing going for us!"

The fact is that Noline was not someone else. She was Noline. The more I tried to push her into one role or another, the more she dug in her heels. I felt trapped, but the trap was of my own making. I was seeking my own selfish ambition, not the welfare of the Kingdom of God. Hindsight is always 20/20. I see it clearly, now that we have matured and allowed the Lord to do a deep and lasting work in our lives. I am convinced that had I truly been discipled as a tender shoot, I would have grown into a straight and upright tree. Instead, I bear the scars, twists, and lumpy knots of a tree that experienced some hard times — not to mention what I did to the trees around me.

Growing Doubts

It is amazing to realize that the same character-

and in our ministry. For the first time, I began to close my spirit to Noline. When this happened, both of us sensed a deep dread coming over our relationship, as we each asked ourselves the secret question, "Could I have made a mistake? Did I marry the wrong person?"

For the next few years, I burdened God with my complaint, "Why didn't You give me someone who would be compatible with my ministry?"

Noline's cry was, "Lord, why did I have to marry a preacher? I was in love with the boy down the road, not this self-righteous minister."

I became very proficient at closing my spirit to her, and she was powerfully and visibly affected by my rejection. As I shut her out of my affections and ministry activities, she began to feel like she was walking on egg shells. She tried, in every way she could think of, to regain an entrance into my life. Her desperate efforts to reach out to me failed, and I rejected her even more — never realizing that my cold rejection was now pushing her further and further away from me. To survive, she became exclusively preoccupied with her children, a primary defense mechanism against the loneliness she was experiencing in our marriage.

The vicious cycle continued and fed upon itself, and I fell more and more in love with another woman — the local church. I spent most of my time with her, prayed for her, visited her, and was glad

woman — the local church. I spent most of my time with her, prayed for her, visited her, and was glad to be around her. As a result, all of the tension between Noline and me was now focused on the church. In my loneliness, I spent even more time with her, calling on people, visiting the sick, and praying for them. I proudly kept a chart in my office, listing all the visits and sick calls I made.

It made me feel very important and appreciated, as a minister, when, in times of crisis, people thought it necessary to ask for my help in resolving their problems. That can be very intoxicating for a young person, and, since my marriage was not as fulfilling as before, my self-worth was totally wrapped up in this need to be needed. I had not yet learned the invaluable lesson that my validation and acceptance must come from the Lord and not from man.

It is sad to say that I had to be stripped of all the trappings of ministry before I could learn properly learn this lesson. For now, though, Noline and I were on a collision course with sorrow. We had sown the seeds that would bear their inevitable fruit. Storm clouds were gathering.

Chapter 5

Sin and Its Consequences

But each one is tempted when he is drawn away by his own desires and enticed. Then, when desire has conceived, it gives birth to sin; and sin, when it is full-grown, brings forth death.

James 1:14-15

"Yes, I will meet you on the deserted road just north of town at 3:00 p.m. on Wednesday."

I couldn't believe what I was saying! I had just made secret arrangements to meet a woman on my worship team at a secluded place on Wednesday — two days away. Adrenaline made my heart pound uncontrollably, as I remembered every word of that fateful phone call. *"I am actually going to go through with it,"* I thought to myself. Part of me sensed a wild exhilaration, yet there was unmistakable fear mixed with it.

My mind began to race with frantic thoughts: *How can I get out of the house to meet her without lying to Noline? Maybe I should call her back and cancel this meeting! No, I couldn't do that now. What would she think of me?* So I remained committed to the meeting that I knew would end in adulterous betrayal. I closed up the church office and tried to lock the door, but my hands shook uncontrollably. I wondered if Noline would detect what was going on by my nervous attitude. *I'll have to hide it well,* I thought.

Wednesday seemed like it was an eternity away. My trips to the office were now empty acts of routine, with no productivity and no joy in my work. I walked around like a caged lion, one moment dreading the coming of Wednesday, and the next moment feeling overwhelmed with excitement and eagerness to act out this illicit romance. Why was sin so pleasurable when I hated the way it made me feel inside? I couldn't pray. I couldn't read. What was I going to do for a Sunday sermon?

When Wednesday finally arrived, I made my usual exit from the house early in the morning and made a few calls here and there. My mind was racing ahead several hours to the time when we were to meet at our scheduled rendezvous. The day dragged on until the fateful moment finally arrived. When I set out for the place, I knew I was doing something terribly wrong, but I preferred to yield to the raging passions within me. My thoughts raced, as I drove away from the church, and continued racing uncontrollably until I reached the rendezvous point and parked at the side of the road. I felt conspicuous sitting alone in my parked car in that deserted area of town. No one ever parked there with good intentions. While I waited, I wondered about the woman I was to meet, and I thought about my wife and children.

This is totally crazy! I thought. *What if someone I know drives by and sees me here?* In fact, a truck did actually drive by, and I could feel the cold stares of its occupants. *They must know,* I thought. I must have looked guilty, because I know I surely felt guilty! Suddenly her car turned the corner, and I thought, *She is here!* as my heart began pounding in my chest. This was for real! It was really happening! There was no turning back now.

Adultery Begins with a Seed

In the 70s, most pastors were expected or even required to be the preacher, the pray-er, the prophesier, the janitor, and the song leader of the church. I am not naturally talented as a musician, but much of my time was spent "working" in the music department. To this day, I don't know who actually initiated the relationship between me and this lady, who was one of the church musicians, but I believe that the relationship was nurtured to fruition by a mutual and continual flirtation with the eyes.

Today, I believe that had Noline and I maintained a solid and strong marriage, we could and would have destroyed that seed of lust when it was still just a thought. Unfortunately, we did not have a healthy relationship at the time, and I didn't know about curbing my thought life (even though I was a preacher). I enjoyed and even relished the idea that someone else found me attractive. I looked for that flirtatious eye contact again, the very next music practice after I had first noticed it. Sure enough, it was still there, and I responded in turn.

The next Sunday, at the end of the morning service, Noline and I took our usual places at the back of the church to shake hands with everyone as they went out of the church. I made sure I was placed so as to intercept the admiring musician, and it happened just as I had planned. As she was leaving, she gave my hand a double squeeze, and confirmed it with an unmistakable look in her eyes and a slight curved smile of her lips.

To anyone else, the exchange probably wouldn't have amounted to anything. Since I had been entertaining lustful thoughts, though, I knew exactly what her message was. This woman was responding to my improper interest with signals that said, "I would like to see you some time." I felt the blood rush to my head so quickly that I was glad I was partially turned away from Noline.

In the days that lay ahead I "worked" even more closely with the music department, thus forming a "soul-tie" between me and the musician. A soul-tie is formed when you allow yourself to be involved with someone of the opposite sex, whether it is spiritually, emotionally, or mentally. After that lengthy period of working, talking, and cultivating a relationship, the unseen bond between this woman and myself was set. I had laid the foundation. Now I began to make plans and to take steps to do what I had promised my wife, before God, on our wedding day, that I would never do. I had said that I would *forsake all others*. I had broken my solemn vow by allowing this relationship to grow, and I would go on breaking my sacred covenant as I built walls of lies and deceit to protect my sin.

Our meeting on that deserted road led to the inevitable. My sinful thoughts led me to willingly commit adultery. Deluded and unrepentant, we made plans to meet again. The vicious cycle was strengthened, and the temporary pleasure of sin got a death grip on my mind and heart. My conscience was paralyzed by its power. I could not and would not break loose from its grip. I was learning the hard way that adultery is one of the devil's most deadly tools of destruction.

The Consequences of Sin

My sin began to kill my spiritual vibrancy with God, it began to erode my relationships with the congregation under my care, and it even began to destroy friendships with those closest to me. I was discovering the painful truth that adultery produces unbearable hurt and pain, leaving in its wake a destroyed marriage and a destroyed ministry.

As the affair continued, Noline had her suspicions, but I kept up a suitable wall of denials. The truth was that it didn't take me long to see that I was losing more than I was gaining by the relationship, and that realization gave me a feeling of desperation. The Word of God now seemed dry to me, and I felt I could no longer "look God in the face," so I naturally avoided my prayer time with Him.

The Hound of Heaven Comes After Me

In the end, the pressure of my wayward life-style became unbearable. The precious Holy Spirit, the "Hound of Heaven," would not leave me alone. I was so deeply wracked with conviction and overwhelmed with guilt that I mysteriously became impotent. Strangely, this malady only manifested with the other woman, not with Noline, and I was embarrassed and humiliated by it.

It was more than that, however. Things were happening that caused a genuine fear to set into my heart. One day, just before the morning service, I was startled by a vision or dream an elderly lady of the church related to me. She said she had dreamed that an adulteress dressed in black was trying to get into the church. I could barely choke out a response. "That's interesting," I said, "I will pray and ask the Lord what it means." We had scarcely finished our conversation when the musicians walked out onto the platform. When they did, I froze and had to stop and catch my breath. I could not believe my eyes, as *she* walked out to take her position with the music team, wearing a long, flowing black dress. That day I thought to myself, *My days are numbered.* I had the sense that sooner or later God was going to expose my sin.

On another occasion, I was at a conference when I met an acquaintance, an intercessor who lived in another city. She told me the Lord had awakened her in the middle of the night to pray and intercede for me. She said the Lord gave her a scripture verse for me. It was when Jesus warned Peter, *"Simon, Simon, Satan has asked to sift you as wheat"* (Luke 22:31). Then she asked me if everything was all right and if there was anything that she could pray for on our behalf. I suddenly wanted to get out of there fast. Things were getting too close for comfort.

With the decline of my spiritual life so obvious and the constant insistence of the Holy Spirit, suddenly my double life was no longer fun or exhilarating and I desperately wanted to be free of the heavy load of deception I was carrying around every day.

Confession

I finally came to the conclusion that if I didn't confess, God would openly expose my sin. I rather expected Him to send a messenger like Nathan, the prophet who had the courage to point his bony finger at King David and say, *"Thou art the man!"* (2 Samuel 12:7). How many more chances would I get? It was then, in total desperation, that I dumped the whole sorry mess on Noline, like a garbage truck emptying its putrid load.

I had no idea what to expect from her. Perhaps I was hoping she would be strong enough (or numb enough) to say, "Okay! Let's pray and then get some help for you." Well, Noline didn't do that. Instead of bailing me out, she went to pieces, with uncontrollable sobbing, and wouldn't let me near her. She shrugged off every attempt to reconcile and, finally, bolted out of the house. I decided not to follow her, thinking that she needed some time and space to assimilate and digest the revelations of the past hour.

When three hours had passed, with no sign of Noline, I panicked. The kids were hungry and crying for Mommy. It was getting dark. "Oh, God," I cried in desperation, "please don't let her do anything foolish." I settled the kids and called in the baby sitter. I decided to drive to my parents' home to see if she had gone there. My next plea was, "O Lord, please don't let Noline tell my parents." My thoughts bounced wildly between dread and self-preservation. It was the reaction of a desperate and hurting person, who has been caught in a terrible sin.

Noline was capable of doing anything, at this point, and, as much as I did not want things to get out of hand, I had to recognize that they were already out of control. I was watching my life come apart at the seams before my very eyes.

On the way to my parents' home, I stopped by the church. Perhaps Noline had taken refuge in the House of God. When I pulled up and walked into the quiet serenity of the sanctuary, I heard muffled sobs coming from the direction of the nursery. I opened the door slightly and found Noline curled up in a fetal position on the floor, heaving and sobbing uncontrollably.

My heart went out to her, but I was totally helpless to act. What could I do to comfort her? After all, I was the one who had caused all her pain and suffering. After a while, I asked her to get up and come home. She did, but she would not look at me or talk to me. That was the longest and most painful night of our marriage. A great chasm was opened between, us as we lay on opposite sides of our bed, each engulfed in a private hell of pain and loneliness. The damage was done.

The next day, Noline's only request was that I call the superintendent of our denomination and let him know the circumstances of my adultery. I knew that the call would end our ministry in the city and possibly anywhere else, but I made up my mind to follow through with it, no matter what the consequences. I decided I would do whatever the church officials asked of me. At this point, I desperately wished that the whole affair had never taken place, and that there was some way of punishing myself for the wrong doing. I sincerely wanted to make amends and somehow "appease" the Lord, Noline, and my own guilty conscience. Unfortunately, there was nothing I could think of to undo this entanglement of lies and betrayal.

Mercy, at this point, seemed unobtainable, a gift not even worthy of my consideration. Resignation, exhaustion, and defeat were my sole companions. Instead of running to God, the way I had preached so often to others, I found myself running from Him.

Human nature is so strange. It is always trying to find its own way to God. The strength of the flesh is rooted in pride. Even when it is humbled to the lowest depths, it still holds you captive in its grip.

After I had notified the denomination officials, we packed our furniture and made plans to move to the city where Noline's parents now lived. None of the locals was told the real reason for our departure, only that we had decided to move. As I look back on those days, I realize that the only way my superiors in the church knew to handle the situation was to release us and find someone else to pastor the church. Unfortunately, that meant that nothing was settled for us. Most serious of all, for me, was the fact that the seeds of sexual impurity continued to germinate within, and no amount of remorse or regret could seem to stem the insidious growth. Moving us to a new location only transplanted the crop to a new harvest field.

I was learning the hard way about sin and its consequences.

Chapter 6

Confession and Forgiveness

Confess your trespasses to one another, and pray for one another, that you may be healed.

James 5:16

NOLINE:

The day started out like any other day, with my daily routine of looking after the children, cleaning, cooking, and answering the telephone. Around four o'clock in the afternoon, I was busy working in the kitchen when Neil came in and started talking. I half-heartedly listened as I continued to prepare for supper. He seemed awkward as he stood there, and that was very unlike him. I realized later that I should have sensed what was coming. He suddenly became very serious and said, "Noline, we need to talk."

I looked up from my meal preparations and focused carefully on Neil's face. As the man I'd been married to for four and a half years began to stammer forth his confession, I felt my whole world shatter into a million pieces. I listened in shocked horror as he confessed to me that he had been "involved" with a lady in our church. It didn't take me long to realize that by "involved" Neil meant he had been having an adulterous affair with her.

I never knew that a person could have so many thoughts going through their head at the same time. Mine was spinning. I felt unbearably sick, and my only consolation was that I finally knew why the last year had been so difficult for us. It was only much later that I realized that perhaps it was because things had been going so badly between us that this horrible thing happened. But I could not think clearly at this moment. Thoughts rushed by in whirls, mixing together as they passed.

How could I cope with this? These things just weren't supposed to happen to people who loved the Lord. Why us? Neil and I had been childhood sweethearts. We were perfect for each other. We had practically grown up together, we had shared our bed and our lives together, we had ministered together, and we had brought lovely children into the world. Now this! I kept thinking, *This only happens to other people — not to us!*

No words could express how angry and hurt I felt; yet, at the same time, I felt strangely detached from it all. I bluntly asked Neil what he wanted to do. "Do you want to carry on the relationship with the other woman? Do you want a divorce?" My mind formed so many other questions that I just could not verbalize at the moment: "Why? What made you do this? How could you do this to me?" Was he that unhappy in our relationship? Wasn't I fulfilling his needs? Was there something wrong with me as a woman? I was devastated.

How could I have been so blind? I guess I felt I could always trust Neil, but now I realized I had kept my head buried in the sand all the time this had been going on. I suddenly felt trapped and claustrophobic in that small kitchen with Neil. I didn't want him near me, didn't want him to touch me or to see me cry. Desperately needing space to gather my thoughts, I asked Neil to go tend to the children and leave me alone for a while. Once he was out of sight, I ran out of the kitchen, down the driveway, and onto the road. I walked and walked, overwhelmed by my emotions. I searched my devastated heart, "Where do I turn? What do I want? With whom can I talk?" On and on I walked until I reached the church. There I felt I could find the solace and comfort I so earnestly needed from my heavenly Father. Unlike my husband, *He* would not let me down.

Conflicting Thoughts

My thoughts were terribly contradictory in the days and weeks that followed Neil's clumsy confession. I desperately tried to sort them all out, but the process seemed impossible. At the same time I hated him for hurting me and wanted desperately to get back at him in some way, I also blamed myself for everything that had happened. Each of my shortcomings, which I knew I should have corrected long ago, now vividly came to mind. As a wife, homemaker, and full-time mother, I had chosen to build my life around my family and home rather than support Neil in the ministry, as he had desired. I was sure now that this had been a mistake and I chided myself endlessly.

Still, as much as I had resisted being crafted into the person he so much wanted me to be, I felt at times that I had actually allowed him to go too far in this regard. I had trusted him too much, relied on him too much. I had, indeed, allowed him to force me to assume the identity he had hand-crafted for me to best impress the church congregation This had to end. I must become an independent woman. I could no longer trust him and was foolish to have trusted him in the past.

I had looked to Neil not only as my husband and friend, but also as my pastor. I had trusted him to handle correctly the Word of God, which he seemed to know so well. Now I was sure that he had used the Word treacherously, for his own purposes, to dismiss any caution or intuitive feeling I may have had about his conduct during the period of his illicit affair.

Confession and Forgiveness

I felt totally robbed of all self-confidence and so stupid that I could not do anything right. *At least,* I told myself, *that is what Neil thinks of me.* But I wasn't going to be stupid any longer. I had been the perfectly submissive wife, totally dependent on my husband, but no more. I was ashamed and humiliated and determined that he would pay for all my hurt.

The Choice To Forgive

Faithfully, the Holy Spirit began ministering to my spirit. He began with the question, "Do you want this marriage?" As usual, He had gone right to the heart of the matter. Well, I knew I really did love Neil, and I wanted all this mess to be over, but how could I forgive him for what he had done? There were days when I felt that I hated Neil for doing this to me. I never wanted him to touch me again, or ever again see me naked. I avoided all direct physical contact with him, and our limited conversations were filled with an angry tone.

With his adultery now out in the open, I had a rod of unforgiveness that I could wield over him; and I sensed that if I forgave Neil immediately, I would lose this power, and he would go back to being dominant over me. It was a real struggle for me to let go and forgive him.

But the Holy Spirit knew my heart and continued to speak to me. He was not interested in making me happy. More importantly, He wanted me healed. "Forgive your husband," came the gentle, but continuous prompting of the Holy Spirit.

All the forgiveness scriptures that I had memorized as a child in Sunday School came flooding back to me. Those principles had been reinforced during our Bible college days. I believed them, and I knew in my heart that eventually I would have to come to terms with these struggles. At the moment, however, my emotions were in upheaval.

Neil had done the right thing in confessing his wrongdoing. This was the first step toward healing. In so doing, he was reaching out for help, wanting to be freed from his trap. Now I needed to do the right thing and forgive him.

Neil had not done his part wisely. He had just blurted out his confession, with no prayerful preparation on his part and no waiting on the Holy Spirit for His timing. He had taken no opportunity for us to pray together, or to seek the Lord together before he began confessing. He had just opened the floodgate, and I was caught in the torrent. Even though I had survived the initial shock of the moment, I still felt dismembered from the bombshell.

Now, however, the ball was in my court, and it was up to me what I would do with it. I had heard someone say that unforgiveness is like picking up a burning coal from a fire and throwing it at the one who has wounded you. The only one who gets burned is you! The flame of rage inside me seemed to be the only weapon I had at the moment. Neil didn't know how to react to it, so he kept his distance. Slowly I began to realize that my rage was also isolating me from the Lord. Deep in my heart I knew the Holy Spirit was right. I had to forgive my husband or this anger and resentment would smother my spiritual existence.

I got on my knees and, as best as I could, I prayed a prayer of forgiveness for both Neil and the other woman. As I stood up, instead of the release I was expecting, I was still flooded with thoughts of anger towards them. I felt I hated them and wanted something terrible to happen to them. I must have tried to forgive them several times over the next few weeks, each time I had the same results. Anger and resentment still filled my heart.

Divorce Is Recommended

At this point, I finally confided in someone I felt I could trust, someone who I thought could give me some sound counsel. I was so wounded that when this person mentioned the option of divorce, it sounded to me like a viable alternative. My pride rose up, wanting to save face from the humiliation of my husband's failure. Yes, I thought, this would be an easy way out of my dilemma. I immediately thought of taking the children and renting an apartment in the suburbs.

As tempting as it seemed, though, I still hesitated. Divorce sounded so final, and it would have to be my choice since Neil was not asking for it. I decided to wait and see what the superintendent would say, since I was still insisting that Neil call him. In the meantime, I bought several books I hoped would help me understand what I was going through and started reading on the subject of forgiveness and filling my heart and mind with the Word. The Bible spoke to my heart one particular morning in my devotions:

> *"For if you* [Noline] *forgive people* [Neil and the other woman] *their trespasses - that is, their* [Neil and the other woman's] *reckless and willful sins, leaving them, letting them go and giving up resentment - your* [Noline's] *heavenly Father will also forgive you* [Noline].
> *"But if you* [Noline] *do not forgive others* [Neil and the other woman] *their trespasses - their* [Neil and the other woman's] *reckless and willful sins, leaving them, letting them go and giving up resentment - neither will your* [Noline's] *Father forgive you* [Noline] *your* [Noline's] *trespasses."* Matthew 6:14-15 AMPLIFIED

Until that moment I had been thinking that forgiveness was a feeling. If I still felt I hated the two of them after praying for them (and I did), then I felt I had not really forgiven them. I learned that day, however, that forgiveness is an act of my will, not a feeling. The very moment I first prayed and forgave them, the transaction was completed — as far as God was concerned. It was my own heart that condemned me through my thoughts and feelings. The morning this truth became a reality to me, I knew I had forgiven Neil and the other woman — no matter what my feelings were at the moment.

A Root of Bitterness

The time I had spent in unforgiveness and resentment had opened the door to yet another problem. I had allowed a seed of bitterness to fall to the ground and germinate. I did not know this until one night, as I lay in bed with my back toward Neil, the Spirit whispered to me, "You have it in your power to save this marriage, if you are willing to tear out this small root of bitterness." I thought of the teaching in Hebrews:

Pursue peace with all men, and holiness, without which no one will see the Lord: looking diligently lest anyone fall short of the grace of God; lest any root of bitterness springing up cause trouble, and by this many become defiled;

Hebrews 12:14-15

When a root is small, it is easy to pull up. The longer it grows, however, the harder it is to uproot. I knew that if I refused to deal with the bitterness in my heart, it would grow and invade every area of my life, affecting me, the children, and everyone else with whom I came in contact. Bitterness would eventually crush any feeling that remained between Neil and me and would make reconciliation impossible.

I had been around some bitter people before and found that it was not a pleasant experience. After being in their presence for just a few minutes, I always felt dirty and defiled. They seemed to have a way of spewing out their resentment in every conversation. I knew in my heart that I had every potential of becoming just like them, and the thought frightened me.

Was I willing to deal with this root now? I knew I didn't want the bitterness, but I wasn't sure I was ready to give up my final hold over Neil. Could I lay down my offense? Ultimately I realized that bitterness would keep me imprisoned without reprieve, forever chained to what had happened in the past. Finally, knowing that any other course would only bring more pain, I opened my heart to the Lord and emptied out all the pain and bitterness at the foot of the cross. Completely engulfed in the wonderful peace that settled over me, I thought, *Well, that is the end of that. Now maybe I can get some sleep.*

Confession and Forgiveness

The Longest Journey

Then the Holy Spirit again spoke to my heart, "I want you to do something else: take your husband in your arms and just hold him." Well, it was one thing to release the bitterness, but this was going too far. Surely I did not have to act on this! Wasn't it enough that I had been obedient in prayer to the Lord? What God was asking me to do would definitely take away all the power I had over my husband. Even worse, I knew he would want to resume sexual relations with me, and I didn't know if I was ready for that just yet. I don't know how long I wrestled with the Lord, but eventually I became willing to do what He required of me.

Neil had his back to me. Inch by dreadful inch, I moved across that gulf between us, getting ever closer to him. That move from my side of the bed to his was the longest journey I have ever taken in my life! I felt like I was dying to pride with every inch that I moved closer to him.

After what seemed an eternity in crossing over to Neil's side of the bed, I folded my arms around him and simply held him tight. He woke up, but he had no idea what was happening. He didn't know what the Lord had been doing in my heart, because I had not shared anything with him up to that point. He was too scared to move and just laid in that position all night, for as long as I held him. I have to admit I enjoyed that!

Recovery

Once God had removed the blockage of unforgiveness and the root of bitterness from my heart, I began to pray for Neil and the other woman without anger and resentment. I continued to read books on the subject of forgiveness and filled my mind and heart with the Word. Soon I came to recognize that God loved Neil and that other woman just as much as He loved me. I also recognized that my sin of unforgiveness had been just as wrong as their sin of adultery. Now that I had settled these issues in my heart, I knew I was free to receive a miracle from the Lord for Neil and myself — and for our children and our marriage. We had obeyed God, Neil in the confession of his sin, and I, in forgiveness.

Chapter 7

A Second Deadly Sip

Then Saul said, "I have sinned. Return, my son David. For I will harm you no more, because my life was precious in your eyes this day. Indeed I have played the fool and erred exceedingly."

1 Samuel 26:21

NEIL:

I was so relieved to be forgiven by Noline, to have our marriage return to some semblance of normalcy and to be able to look God in the face once again that I never imagined this thing might happen again at some point. That wasn't possible. Or was it?

Although we were embarrassed by what had happened, we were determined to go on with our lives. Exactly what we were going to do next we didn't know. We had left our first pastorate and were living with Noline's parents in a small community of just over a thousand people. No one knew us there, and it seemed like a good place to let our wounds heal and to have a fresh start. I decided to take some college courses while we sorted things out.

Not long after we moved into the new neighborhood, however, we started meeting people who were looking for a pastor for their small nondenominational group. In just two weeks, we had assumed the pastorate of a new fellowship with twelve members and began holding meetings; and, within months, the fellowship had grown to between sixty and eighty members.

Part of that growth may have been due to the curiosity of the small-town environment, but, for whatever reason, membership continued to grow, and giving and tithing were increasing each week. Within a short time, there were enough funds for us to move into our own home and enjoy life at a more leisurely pace.

The people of the town were wonderful to us. They were impressed with the "big city preacher," and I didn't do anything to dissuade them. I enjoyed the adulation and the authority that adulation gave me.

However, things had not returned to *normal*, in any sense. I still had many questions in my mind about what had happened to me, why, and what I should do about it. My private devotional time had not returned to its previous fervency, and that troubled me; yet I never imagined what was to happen next.

A Second Deadly Sip

Temptation

Temptation found me sitting at the reception table of a wedding I had just attended. My knee inadvertently touched the leg of the single girl who had traveled with us for the occasion. To my surprise, her leg didn't move away. In fact, I distinctly felt her exert pressure my way. I thought perhaps I was mistaken, so I decided to test it. I extended my foot forward and touched hers. Again, I felt a distinct nudge in return.

At that point, I felt that all-too-familiar rush of adrenaline in my body and was sure someone would see that I was flushed in the face. That feeling of excitement mysteriously blocked out the quiet, but urgent voice of the Holy Spirit. I could faintly hear Him saying something about Moses choosing to be mistreated rather than to enjoy the pleasure of sin for a short time, but the words trailed off so that I could not hear the end of the verse. I was too preoccupied with the illicit under-the-table communication.

Intimacy

I found myself longing for the one-and-a-half hour drive home after the wedding. As we drove home through the countryside in the stillness of the night, I ignored all the inner warnings and maneuvered myself to the driver's seat, with the young lady

lady seated next to me. Then, when I was sure that no one could see me, I reached out and took hold of her hand. Her response was immediate and affirmative. She held my hand tightly in hers.

Later that night, we were more passionate, and from then on we took every opportunity possible to meet secretly. Very little time was spent "getting to know each other," and soon I set my mind and passions on formulating a scheme so we could be together for an entire night to consummate our lust. Once again, I set aside the voice of God to willfully yield to my fleshly desires.

We took advantage of my college course schedule to plan our time together. I decided I would tell Noline that I needed to be away for a couple of days to study for upcoming tests. That way I could be at the young woman's house overnight. The course was set. Again, lies and deception were the main tools of my betrayal and self-destruction, and they worked well for me. We met alone in the cover of night and were sexually intimate.

I'm sure every reader will wonder why I hadn't learned my lesson the first time, and I wondered that too. I wondered what was wrong with me. I thought that I had repented of my sin and that it would not reoccur. Hadn't I put it all under the blood of Jesus? I thought I had. What was going on. Questions such as these swirled through my mind constantly.

This second deadly sip was certainly not God's

fault. He had done His best to keep me from falling again, but my flesh refused to cooperate, refused to accept what I knew to be best for me in the long run. I was consumed with the moments of temporary gratification I could have in secret.

This second affair, which occurred so soon after the first, did not last long. One of the major contributing factors which led to its end was a dream I had. I have never been one given to dreams or great revelations; they must be very clear before I venture to say that they are from God, but this dream was real, and clear; and, to this day, I still remember the minute details of it, as though it had just happened.

The Dream

I dreamed I was walking down a hospital corridor. A little way ahead was a group of people whom I knew (although I couldn't remember later who they were). When I reached the door to a hospital room, they tried to keep me from going in. Somehow, I knew that Noline was the one in that room; I pushed through the friends at the door and walked on into the room. I made my way to the left side of the bed. A nurse was standing on the right side. The bedsheet had been pulled over Noline's face, and when I reached out to pull back the sheet, the nurse exclaimed, "No! Don't do it! She's dead!"

Ignoring her request, I pulled the covers back

and, when I saw that ashen-gray face, with all the life blood drained from it, I began to sob. I was overcome with gut-wrenching sobs, both in the dream and physically, in my sleep. It literally felt like someone had reached into my inner being and turned me inside out!

In the dream, I suddenly took hold of Noline's hand, pulled her limp body up to a sitting position, and said, "Noline, in the name of Jesus, arise and live!" In that instant, she awoke from her death sleep and was alive again. It was at that point that my dream came to a sudden end.

I was instantly awake and alert and, at that same moment, these words forcefully invaded my mind and thoughts: "I am killing my wife's love for me through this adultery!" Again and again, as if a continuous tape recording were playing in my head, I heard the words, "I am killing my wife's love for me through this adultery!" I didn't discover the dream's full meaning for four more years. Then the Lord revealed to me that the "gut wrenching" was our "one flesh" relationship that I was killing. From that day on I sought for ways to end my illicit affair.

When the affair had ended, there was so much pain and hurt still lingering from the last time I had confessed to adultery, that I thought bringing a second case to the surface would be craziness on my part. I had learned the hard way that confession without healing leaves one with a hardness of heart and critical unbelief. This may lead to the opinion that "nothing really works," and it can create mistrust both in the ability of God and His servants to bring about a true and lasting healing in your life.

One thing was sure: I was a *"wretched man"* and understood all too well the words of the Apostle Paul:

> *What a wretched man I am! Who will rescue me*
> *from this body of death?*
> *So then, I myself ... am ... a slave to the law of sin.*
> Romans 7:24-25

What Was My Problem?

If I thought I had unanswered questions before, now they had become a veritable plague on my mind and would not leave me day or night. Terms that I had been hearing in certain circles began to flood my mind. Did I have some sort of "generational curse" that had come down through my family line? Had the "secret sins" of my father or forefathers before him carried over into my life? Could my uncontrolled lust be a symptom of "demonic possession"? Could I have been the victim of "the transference of spirits," where a compulsive lust problem jumped into me from some other spiritual leader in authority over me? If I was suffering some sort of demonic influence, who could I possibly talk to about it? And could a Christian even be demon possessed? I knew that all of these theories were extremely controversial within the church and I was left pondering. I had a lot of questions, but not many answers.

In the end, the answer seemed to be simply that I had been tempted and had not been willing to resist the temptation. Period! I had come to the conclusion that it is wrong to wrangle over these doctrinal differences concerning demonic influence in the life of a believer. Whatever the truth of any of the controversial and divisive concepts concerning Satan and his legions of demons, we can be sure that Jesus destroyed the power of the devil at Calvary; and, in the Name of Jesus, every spirit must flee from us, whatever our problem happens to be and whatever caused it in the first place.

Repentance or Remorse?

Had my repentance from the first sin been genuine? I thought it had. Or had I only felt guilty and embarrassed after confessing to Noline? Did I have a sincere abhorrence of sin? Or, when the penalty of sin was removed and things seemed to be flowing smoothly again, was it easy for me to forget how I had suffered the first time and do it all over again? Something was wrong, and I had to know what it was.

I had taken a second deadly sip. Now I would have to live with the consequences.

Chapter 8

The Continuing Soul-tie

And Dinah the daughter of Leah, which she bare unto Jacob, went out to see the daughters of the land. And when Shechem the son of Hamor the Hivite, prince of the country, saw her, he took her, and lay with her, and defiled her. And his soul clave unto Dinah the daughter of Jacob, and he loved the damsel, and spake kindly unto the damsel ... . And Hamor communed with them, saying, The soul of my son Shechem longeth for your daughter: I pray you give her him to wife.

Genesis 34:1-3, 8 KJV

NEIL:

Little is understood about the unseen spiritual vice-grip commonly known by many as a "soul-tie." Genesis expresses it in these words: *"his soul clave unto Dinah."* A "soul-tie" is a mystical union created when two people are united in the sexual act. The soul-tie was created by God as a gift to married couples, since through the sexual act (reserved by

God for marriage), He intended to unite a man and a woman in a bond so powerful that they could live together the rest of their lives. When men and women have sexual relations outside of marriage, the soul-tie is created, nevertheless. So, although the lady and I had mutually agreed to terminate our relationship, and although my wife and I decided to move to another town for ministry purposes, this did not solve my problem, because that soul-tie, created in our moments of sexual intimacy, could not be so easily broken.

I was very happy to be moving because now we would get away from the town and away from the woman. By now I recognized my weakness in this regard and wanted to deny myself any opportunity to resume the sinful relationship. Staying where we were, I considered, would be dangerous to my soul, because the woman involved, whom I began to think of as "the alien woman," had, by now, made herself a close personal friend of our family. Although I was determined that what was finished was finished, she was still attracted to me and kept as close to our family as she could.

After we moved, "the alien woman" continued to write us, and, after a while, suggested that she visit us — which she did, traveling some distance. Our work in this new town was, again, pastoral, as before; but there was an added responsibility — a Christian school. When "the alien woman" visited us, she hit it off right away with our school principal, so much so that the principal offered her a job. That fact severely distressed me. *Oh no!* I thought. *Just when things should have been getting better, they take a sudden turn for the worse!* There was nothing I could do, so, rather than panic, I decided to face whatever happened with a determination not to, under any circumstances, allow the past to bring me back into bondage to it's power. That determination would not be easy to keep.

When a hidden soul-tie is in operation, even those close to the person affected often cannot understand the strange behavior they witness. It often remains a mystery to them, unless the Holy Spirit reveals it, how or why someone has such control over your life. Once, when "the alien woman" was in our home, she asked that a chair be placed in a certain part of the living room. I immediately got up and moved the chair. Later that night, Noline asked me why I had let our friend treat me that way, especially since I wouldn't have done the same thing for my own wife. What could I say? I was entangled in a very deep-set soul relationship with the woman, and I did not know how I would ever break free from it.

"The alien woman" accepted my school principal's offer and moved to the city where we were living. She worshipped in our church and taught in our school. It seemed as though I was doomed to live with my sinful past flagrantly displayed before my face every day. In the midst of it all, however, I did manage to keep myself from any close physical relationship with her. But I had no idea how to break the soul-tie that still existed.

Church Conflict

After a time, another pastor and his wife joined us in the work. We thought this couple, who had been close friends of ours for many years, would be ideal co-pastors and ministry partners at that growing church. We were so happy about their coming that we made him the senior pastor of the church. This, however, was the beginning of some very low times in my ministry since the two of us were so much alike that we rubbed each other the wrong way. As problems arose, we tried our best to resolve them so that we could minister smoothly together. Instead, the situation deteriorated. What neither one of us realized at the time was that our difficulties were actually the hand of God about to answer my pleas for help.

However, it was not exactly what I had in mind. I envisioned God working in a far different way; but He knows what He is doing and always does it just right. My preference would have been for God to somehow do a miracle and remove both the co-pastor and the alien woman, but God was about to remove us instead. How wonderful are His ways! This pastor friend, who seemed to be causing me so much grief, was going to be the tool God would use to free me from the past.

The Continuing Soul-Tie

Jesus was able to work with twelve men of varying temperaments and from every walk of life; and even though they had differences of opinion, He was able to mold them into a viable team. Many times, when church leaders are unable to work out their differences, it is because there is sin in the camp. It is never because the Spirit of Christ is incapable of bringing peace to the situation.

If parties are defensive or feel threatened by counsel from others, this may be an indication that sin is present. In this case, I was the problem and couldn't see it. I was convinced that the senior pastor was trying to take the church from us, and it infuriated me. After all, we were there first, and we had invited him! I could think of nothing else. What motive could he have for trying to bring Noline and me under his control? I was fighting for my life and ministry.

Now I realize that the Master Potter was working in my life, and I thank Him. He can use any tool He chooses to do His marvelous work. I am His unworthy clay:

> *I know that nothing good lives in me, that is, in my sinful nature. For I have the desire to do what is good, but I cannot carry it out. For what I do is not the good I want to do; no, the evil I do not want to do—this I keep on doing.*
> Romans 7:18-19 NIV

As yet, I had no understanding of what I was experiencing.

79

NOLINE:

Neil and I were having difficulties with the senior pastor and his wife, the very people we had invited to join us in the work. Ironically, from our perspective, it seemed as if they did not want us in the assembly any more. Neil was taking all this very personally, so I committed myself to pray for him and to ask the Lord if it was His will that we leave. In my early morning devotions, I opened my Bible to Isaiah 53. I knew this chapter contained the prophetic word concerning the crucifixion of Christ, and I thought it was strange that the Lord would direct me there for a word concerning Neil.

If you have ever had a verse jump out at you while you were reading the Bible, you will understand what happened to me that morning. The words that seemed to come alive to me were:

Yet it was the Lord's will to crush him and cause him to suffer, and though the Lord makes his life a guilt offering, he will see his offspring and prolong his days, and the will of the Lord will prosper in his hand.   Isaiah 53:10 NIV

It was as though the Lord said to me, "What is happening to Neil is My doing. Take your hands off him, and let Me complete what I have started in him."

When my family goes through tough times, I instinctively want to stand and fight for them. This was my feeling at the time for Neil. I wanted to fight for his right to work with our church. Yet the Lord was asking me to take my hands off him. I saw how dejected and depressed he felt day after day, and I could do nothing to help him. I had to just stand back and watch my husband be crushed. As the senior pastor put more and more pressure on Neil, all that I could do was pray for him continuously. Thank God that His prophetic word had prepared me for that hour.

Looking back on the situation, I can see how the Lord used the senior pastor as a tool, to chip away at the hardness of my husband's heart. It was like watching someone conduct open-heart surgery on Neil without giving him an anesthetic. He was in terrible pain, and I wanted to go in and save him from this awful ordeal. But I couldn't. The word of the Lord both restrained me and comforted me through the whole process. His assurance to me was that Neil would come out of this "open-heart surgery" alive and changed.

NEIL:

Somehow, in this great struggle, I became convinced that it was all because of my sin. I can't tell you how many times I cried out to God to forgive me, and I believed that I was forgiven; yet I could not face my past. There were occasions when I would sense the anointing of God and rise to the occasion; but, just as I was about to break through, the devil would bludgeon me with the past, saying, "You can't prosper because you have hidden sin in your life." In those moments, I would slump back into a defeatist attitude and take every blow that was directed at me. By receiving such blows, I somehow thought I was doing my part to remedy the situation, some penance for the wrong that I had done.

There was no end to this vicious cycle, and it left me a most miserable man. I knew that the penalty of my sin was under the blood, yet I had no rest, feeling that sin still had me by the throat. I was so desperate that, at one point, I even considered ending my life so my family could be set free from bearing the load and the punishment that I was bringing upon our household and the Body of Christ. This was the lowest ebb of my life.

At this point of my life, one important thing was accomplished by my utter humiliation. I had plenty of time to be introspective and was convinced how utterly helpless I was to bring about my own healing. God would have to do it, and He would do it — in His way and in His time. I was now dependent on Him for the final breaking in my life.

During this dark period in my life, a totally crazy idea came to me, an idea that had its roots in the continuing soul-tie. I knew that "the alien woman" thought very highly of the pastor with whom I was clashing, so, in a desperate bid for some type of victory over him, I decided to visit her apartment. In my twisted thinking, I had determined that if she preferred me over him, I would, in some strange way, have triumphed. As soon as we were alone, I took her in my arms and embraced her. She pushed away and said we should not get involved; and I accepted the rebuke. There was no further romantic contact between us.

Soul-ties bridge across a strange dichotomy. On the one hand, there may be no ongoing physical relationship, as in my case with "the alien woman." Yet, on the other hand, the emotional tie between the two parties may be virtually unending and very strong. I know today that the only way to break any soul-tie with the opposite sex — whether it be emotional, spiritual, or physical — is to be totally transparent to the one closest to you (your spouse).

Noline and I normally kept absolutely nothing hidden between us, and today, should there ever appear to be any overt or covert attraction to the opposite sex, we immediately confer with each other, talk things out, and pray about the matter. In this way, we help each other avoid the sins of the flesh that can gain such power over an individual.

Run Out of Wine

My inner personal struggle, my struggle with the other pastor and my continued soul-tie to the woman were, by now, taking a terrible toll on my life. I was a spiritual and emotional wreck, and this had a devastating effect on our marriage. As far as I was concerned, we had come to the end of the line. Our boat had hit the reef, and we were taking on water fast. We were sinking, and no rescue was in sight.

I was convinced that Noline and I had totally run out of wine. We just didn't have the excitement or the love that we had enjoyed in the past. We were merely existing on the dregs left over in our relationship. Any intoxication with each other was now gone. We were sober, dry, and left with no love to give. Our marriage had become an empty relationship, and we were only staying together because of our obligation and responsibility to the children.

And it was all my fault. The huge wall of lies and deceit I had built up from the past continued to divide us, and there was no "light at the end of the tunnel," nor did any kind of breakthrough lay ahead for us that we could see. It is amazing how every aspect of our walk with God is affected when we are not right spiritually and there is hidden sin in our lives.

The consequence of this hidden sin was directly affecting my ministry, along with any hope that I had for my future. My sermons were as dry as my life, and all of my working relationships in the church leadership were also doomed to failure. I was a man living a lie. Where could I turn?

Chapter 9

Seeking Help

The Lord said, "I have indeed seen the misery of My people in Egypt. I have heard them crying out because of their slave drivers, and I am concerned about their suffering. So I have come down to rescue them from the hand of the Egyptians and to bring them up out of that land into a good and spacious land, a land flowing with milk and honey — the home of the Canaanites, Hittites, Amorites, Perizzites, Hivites, and Jebusites. And now the cry of the Israelites has reached Me, and I have seen the way the Egyptians are oppressing them. So now, go, I am sending you to Pharaoh to bring My people the Israelites out of Egypt.

Exodus 3:7-10

NEIL:

"I wish I could just die! If only I had not sinned, if only I had not dragged my family into this ugly mess!" Life for our family had taken a wrong turn, and I was sure it was all because of my iniquity. How

I hated myself! And in my desperation, I cried out to God.

He always hears the cry of those who truly love him and seek Him. We may not think so at the time. Sometimes it seems that the heavens are of brass and that none of our prayers are penetrating to the throne of God. But even when we feel as though we're not breaking through because of guilt or indwelling sin, or both, God still hears the cry of the contrite heart.

In my hour of greatest desperation, God heard my cry. He saw that I longed to be free and serve Him with the purity and holiness that He required of me. He knew that without a fresh vision, a word of hope, I would not be able to face the future and find His release.

His answer came in the form of a couple's weekend held in our city. Marriage Ministries International was conducting a Leadership Training Weekend (LTW), and by default, it fell to Noline and me to represent our church leadership at the seminar. I was not entirely thrilled at the prospect. Most men never really want to go to these marriage seminars, perhaps because they feel, as I did, that I had told my wife that I loved her on our wedding day, and what more did she want? (Thank God I'm wiser now.) Men are conquerors (we say), and once the marriage relationship is secured, our wives should know that we will always love them. (It sounds so reasonable to the practical male mind.) On the other hand, wives are relational creatures. They will do

almost anything to have their husbands more involved in the marriage relationship with them. What
would this meeting be like?

I'll Go, But No Saran Wrap!

Noline was happy that we were going. I wasn't
so sure, but kept telling myself I would go and "as-
sess the spirit of the ministry" and judge its "Word"
content at the same time. I also set some invisible
boundaries for my own safety. If they crossed the
line, I would leave. I told Noline, "If they get up and
talk about wives meeting their husbands at the door
when they get home from work dressed only in Sa-
ran Wrap, I'm out of there!" I figured it couldn't hurt
to attend. I might, at least, get some new sermon
material. Secretly, I had already prepared myself to
endure many long hours of boring teaching, convinced that I would not have a very good time. How
wrong I was!

I had never heard teaching on covenant like I heard
it at that seminar, and what they said made a lot of
sense. It was also very consistent with Gospel teaching. All the lessons were based totally on God's Word.
I was not bored once, but absorbed lesson after lesson,
as God's Word convicted my heart as to what marriage was all about. At the end of the first evening, I
leaned over to Noline, so that no one else could hear
me, and confided in her that I thought all in all it had
been a very good experience.

How Could I "Spill My Guts" to Strangers?

MMI had prepared a series of thirteen lessons covering every aspect of biblical teaching which could be and should be practically related to marriage. Periodically they would hold a seminar to which they would invite leaders from the various churches and would teach them the thirteen principles in two days, asking them to share with others, in homes and churches, what they had learned, giving one principle each week for thirteen weeks.

At one point during the seminar, the speaker asked each couple what they thought their marriage was like. When they got to me, I found myself unwilling to tell the whole truth and replied, "Our marriage couldn't be better." What a lie!

Well, what did they expect? After all, how could I spill my guts in an open forum in front of a bunch of strangers? No, they would have to be satisfied with the "perfect couple" story. I convinced myself that this had been an honorable approach, if for no other reason than because it would avoid "bringing disrepute" on the church. However, when I thought about it, I had to admit that God doesn't seem to have a problem revealing the whole truth about His servants and prophets in His Word. He often told of their flaws, their failures, their betrayals, and their shortcomings. Apparently it is not God who fears the exposure of sin. It is we who have such fears.

Yet, it seemed better for me, at the time, to lie than to tell the truth or, if I had the option, to say nothing.

Aside from this personal aspect of the seminar, however, I was enjoying it very much, and by the end of the second evening, any lingering skepticism about the seminar had totally evaporated. I was convinced that we had found answers, not only for our own problems, but for many couples in the Body of Christ. A tremendous vision was being birthed in our wounded hearts that weekend, and we could hardly wait for the opportunity to get home and begin teaching our own group what we had learned.

We Are Chosen to Teach Others

Noline and I began teaching our first Married for Life group within two weeks of our initial training. We did it in our own home and invited other couples from the church to attend. Even in our own home setting and with friends, I still could not bring myself to be open and transparent about my past life. Things were about to change, however, because God was hot on my trail!

Not long afterward, Noline and I were invited to accompany and help teach with Mike and Marilyn Phillipps (the Founding Directors of Marriage Ministries International) on a Leadership Training Weekend out of state. When Mike and Marilyn were teaching on the twelfth lesson, "Life Patterns," a great deal of time was spent discussing the passage in the Book of James which deals with the need to confess to each other sins against the marriage:

Therefore confess your sins to each other and pray for each other so that you may be healed.
James 5:16 NIV

The Phillipps brought out the fact that it is *sin* that does the damage in a relationship, not the confession of that sin. They mentioned the error of some in dumping their confession of heinous sin onto their innocent spouse, who then crumple into a broken emotional heap, never to recover. I could understand what they were saying because I had done exactly the same thing to Noline. Because of the horrendous outcome of that confession, I regretted ever telling her.

Because of this most pastors discourage confession of wrongdoing to a spouse for fear that the confession might actually make things worse, even causing divorce. Therefore, they often counsel guilty mates to confess their sin to their pastor and, particularly, to the Lord, put it under the blood of Christ, and go on.

This was my thinking at the time, too; so I had a "dumping" scenario running through my mind the whole time the Phillipps were teaching this particular lesson.

I Saw a Glimmer of Hope

Then, something they said really got my attention. "Your 'one-flesh relationship' was wounded the moment your spouse sinned, not at the time of confession," they told us.

"Wow!" I mumbled under my breath. This really hit home: CONFESSION AND PRAYER WERE FOR HEALING, NOT DESTRUCTION. This was a revelation to me, and my spirit man leapt inside my being. Scales began to fall from my eyes that day; and I saw a glimmer of hope for the first time in five years. During the next few hours, we saw miracles taking place in many couples, as the Spirit of God set them free from indwelling sin.

One couple in particular stood out from all the rest. They came into the meeting room the next morning, and the husband volunteered that the previous night his wife had confessed to him that their eighteen-year-old daughter was not his. She had admitted to her husband that the child had been conceived while he was in the military.

This was a pastor's nightmare! *This is definitely out of order*, I thought, but the big problem with my theology and professional training was that HE WAS FREE; AND *I* WAS NOT! This man told us that for years he just could not get close to his daughter. Now that the power of the devil was broken, he could hardly wait to get home and rebuild the relationship. His joy was phenomenal!

Why Don't You Confess First?

Somehow I sensed that this was my chance to also be free of the guilt I had harbored for so long, and I was anxious for an opportunity to be alone with Noline so that we could talk. I thought I'd test the waters first, though, by asking Noline: "Do you have any hidden sin in your life that you need to confess to me and to God?" I was almost hoping she would say yes. If I could establish that I wasn't the only bad one around, I felt it would help to justify my failure. So if she did confess anything, it would have made it a whole lot easier for me, or so I thought at the time.

To my dismay, she laughed and said, "No," quickly returning the ball to my court when she fired back, "But do you?" I had intended to confess in that moment, but suddenly I was left speechless. My mouth went dry and the words seemed to stick in my throat. "No!" I answered weakly. Now, supposedly we were on a par with each other, since each of us was free of past sin; but, in reality, my sins were only stacking up.

I told myself that the lie was necessary, because of the consequences and the pain of my first confession of adultery. I couldn't forget the turmoil it brought to our marriage and relationship and how long it took us to get over it. There was just no way I could ever do that again. The truth, though, was that I knew what I should do but was just too scared to do it.

The weekend ended without any further resolution to my dilemma. We flew home, and I sank back into darkness. Over and over I relived those days and my opportunity to do the right thing. Over and over I wondered why I had not opened up to these wonderful people who were there to help us. *At least Mike and Marilyn could have kept Noline from killing me*, I told myself sarcastically. But it was no laughing matter. I had missed a great opportunity to be free.

By the time we had taught our fourth Married for Life group, I had an overwhelming longing in my heart to be free from my guilt. Little did I realize how close I was to the greatest encounter with God that I had ever experienced since the moment I was saved and baptized in the Holy Spirit.

A Visit in the Night

One night, not long after that, I could not sleep. I tossed and turned long after we went to bed. It seemed to me I had been struggling to sleep the whole night. At 3:00 a.m., I gave up any hope of sleeping and decided to go downstairs to the basement to pray. I didn't really think I would receive any revelation from God. I doubted that He even wanted to talk to me. The heavens had been like brass now for such a long time. Figuring that I had nothing to lose, I went to my office, got on my knees, and began to pray.

In just a brief moment, the whole office began to glow with the presence of the Lord. I heard the Lord speak to me, not in an audible voice, but into my heart and into my spirit, "Do you like My presence?"

I answered, "Yes, Lord, I've longed for this day. It seems like an eternity since I've heard Your voice."

Then the Lord replied, "Go and tell your wife about the adultery."

My guard went up, and I protested, "I can't!"

Then, just as quickly as the presence of the Lord had come, it left. Dismayed, I cried out, "Lord, I can't live like I have for the past five-and-a-half years!"

Again, the presence of the Lord descended, and my office began to glow once more. Again I heard the voice of the Lord speak to my heart, "Do you like My presence?" and again I answered in the affirmative. Then He said a second time: "Go and tell your wife about the adultery." But I just could not bring myself to do it.

I "reminded" the Lord of the reaction I got the first time I confessed — just in case He had forgotten. The presence of the Lord came and went again several times, as He continued drawing me to Himself and consistently making the same request.

At 5:00 a.m., I finally surrendered to His will, or nearly so. I would confess to Noline, I told the Lord, if He would give me one last fleece. If Noline was up and awake with the light on, I would do it. I was sure I had won. I knew that Noline was not a morning person. She is like a deep sea submarine; it takes her a long time to surface. I was pretty confident that she would be asleep at 5:00 a.m., in the middle of winter, when it was still pitch black outside. There was no way she would be awake.

I turned off the light in my office, climbed the stairs to the kitchen, and confidently began to walk down the passage to the master bedroom. My heart suddenly leaped, and my mouth became instantly dry, as waves of fear gripped me. I could not believe my eyes! Noline's light was on! I could see it through the crack at the bottom of the door. *God has tricked me!* I thought. Just seconds ago I had been so confident, and now my hands were shaking. At first, I was only able to rattle the door instead of opening it. All of my courage had just dissipated into thin air.

She Won't Be Able To Stab Me

As I cracked the door a few inches, hoping to see a familiar sleeping form, Noline looked up from the bed where she had been sitting up reading her Bible. I smiled weakly, as I felt all the strength going out of my limbs, but I managed to say, "Honey, would you like to lie down here on the carpet and pray for awhile?" I thought to myself, *If I can get her onto the floor, she won't be able to stab me with the scissors.* Isn't it amazing what goofy thoughts we have in times of crisis?

A few minutes into our prayer time, I said to

Noline, "I have something I would like to share with you." Then, for the first time in more than five long, tormenting years, through broken confession, my secret sin was brought into the light. Noline burst into tears; but this time, to my surprise, I was crying too. I hadn't shed a tear in years. We talked and cried for what seemed to be ages. Noline ended our talk by laying her loving hands on me and praying a prayer of forgiveness and healing for me.

NOLINE:

God is so faithful to us. His Word is our strength in times of weakness. Little did I know that God was chipping away at Neil's heart to get to the depth of past sin in his life! Early one morning when I awoke, I discovered that Neil was already up and was in his office for his devotions. I had no idea how long he had been gone, but I turned on the light and began to read my Bible. At about 5:00 a.m. Neil came back to bed and suggested that we have some prayer together.

While we were praying, he lobbed an emotional grenade my way, pouring out his heart and confessing that God had met him in his office in a supernatural way. In this meeting with the Lord, God asked Neil to confess to me that he had been involved in a second adulterous affair only a short while after the first, and that he had hidden it from me all this time.

Seeking Help

I was stunned and shocked. When he told me who the woman was, I nearly died! She had become one of our best friends, had stayed in our home, shared meals with us, and even watched our little children while we were away. I had trusted her. How could she deceive me in this way?

I burst into tears, but, unexpectedly, so did Neil. I had not seen him cry for ages. We wept and prayed together, and he asked me to lay hands on him, to pray for him, to forgive him, and to bind the spirit of lust that had oppressed him. God had been faithful to prepare me in His Word, so I did not fall to pieces as I had done five years earlier. The Holy Spirit had deposited an inner peace and confidence within me.

What really helped me was Neil's attitude. Not only was he repentant, but I saw a brokenness in him that I had not seen before. A couple of days later, I felt that it was the time to share the scripture I had been standing on during the time God had been working in Neil's life. We had been through a training weekend with Marriage Ministries International, and had completed four thirteen-week groups. This gave us a chance to work on many of the principles in the manual and helped me not to be devastated by this revelation as I was the first time.

Even though I was prepared by the Lord, there was still a wounding. The same old inadequate feeling, that I had been unable to fulfill my husband's needs, welled up inside me. Anger, unforgiveness, and resentment filled my mind. I knew I would immediately have to allow God to begin healing my wounds and disappointment. Despite the pain, I was relieved that the truth was out, and we could now face the future together.

NEIL:

That night, Noline and I made a lifelong agreement between us: We gave each other the exclusive right to talk and to ask questions about anything, anytime. My personal resolution to my wife was simple: "Just as I was part of the problem, now I will be part of the solution." I would never allow the devil to lie to me and tell me that my wife was accusing me any time she brought up the subject of sexual temptation or sin. She would have many questions, and would not always require an answer. Sometimes she would only need me to hold her close, assure her of my love, and pray for her.

It is not enough to confess wrongdoing to a spouse and then expect them to never again bring up the subject. Sure, it's under the blood now. Sure, it's in the sea of God's forgetfulness. That spouse who has been wounded needs opportunity to clear up the matter in his or her own heart and mind. If not, he or she will become a prisoner to the pain of the confession, finding no escape from the disappointment, wounds, and bruises that have been inflicted. This innocent victim is literally held captive to the vivid imagination of what he or she believes went on between the spouse and the other person. This is not only unfair, it is also unjust! For example, Noline needed to know who the other woman was so that she would not look upon *all* other women with suspicion in the future.

One thing we did not do. Although we did speak freely about when and where my sin took place, we both agreed that the details of the actual sin would never be discussed. I was ashamed of what I had done, and preferred to forget the gory details, while Noline did not want vivid pictures of my sin painted in her mind. And then we left it with God.

Healing takes time, but God is a Healer. Jesus said that He had come to heal those who were *bruised* (Luke 4:18). Bruises sometimes take a long time to heal, and during the time they are healing, the slightest bump on the affected area can be extremely painful, much like being injured all over again. As it is in the natural, so it is in the spiritual. Both physical and emotional bruises require time for proper healing.

Jesus Didn't Promise Amnesia

To this day, I do not know if Noline and I are one hundred percent healed from the past. All I know is that we can touch the affected areas without feeling pain. The bruises are gone, and only the scars remain. Jesus did not say He would give us amnesia, but He did say that He would heal our pain and our bruises.

The sin that had separated us had been removed, and we knew God would begin to fashion us as one again. After I exposed the adultery, the Lord brought to mind a prophecy that we were given years before that declared:

God will take you like two hands of a clock and bring you into cadence. He will make you one. People will see you, that you are in step with God, and in step with each other.

I felt that the fulfillment of that prophecy must now be eminent.

I was not totally restored yet. I had taken an important first step, but other steps awaited me. Although I had confessed my sin to Noline, I had not completely dealt with the pattern of deception that had dominated my life for years. No matter how I justified myself and fooled others, I could not fool my own heart or the heart of God. I had been forgiven by God, but I needed to be refashioned on the Potter's wheel. The Master Potter had a lot more work to do in my heart. I was glad, though, that I had sought His help.

Chapter 10

Crushing Humiliation and Caring Rehabilitation

Everyone who falls on that Stone will be broken to pieces, but he on whom it falls will be crushed.
Luke 20:18 NIV

NEIL:

If only the confession of my sin had dealt with the *cause* of it and not just the *results*! The King James Version says, *"It will grind him to powder."* We have two choices with God: either we choose to be broken by the Word, or He will *grind [us] to powder.* This may sound pretty gruesome to modern ears, but God, the Master Potter, cannot fashion us into the vessels He desires if there are lumps in the clay.

When we willingly allow ourselves to be thoroughly broken, through the convicting power of the Holy Spirit and through His Word, God can mold us without putting us through the "grinding process." This, of course, is the better way. Alas, it was not to be in my case, for I had consistently refused to fully obey the many promptings by the Holy Spirit.

Isaiah the prophet declared:

Therefore, this is what the Holy One of Israel says: "Because you have rejected this message, relied on oppression and depended on deceit, this sin will become for you like a high wall, cracked and bulging, that collapses suddenly, in an instant. It will break in pieces like pottery, shattered so mercilessly that among its pieces not a fragment will be found for taking coals from a hearth or scooping water out of a cistern. Isaiah 30:12-14 NIV

My wall of lies and deceit was about to be crushed. Oh, if only I had listened to the Lord at the first rebuke, at the first chastening of His gentle hand; then I would not have to go through this crushing! In the natural, it looked like I faced total disaster, but I had to trust the Lord that He knew what He was doing and that His promise would take me through the breaking period. Even when my whole world began to crumble in the open arena of public scrutiny, I had the promise that He was with me. Again and again, I would hear Him speak and I would know that I was on the right road.

Although the Lord gives you the bread of adversity

> *and the water of affliction, your teachers will be*
> *hidden no more; with your own eyes you will see*
> *them. Whether you turn to the right or to the left,*
> *your ears will hear a voice behind you, saying,*
> *"This is the way; walk in it."*
>
> Isaiah 30:20 NIV

The public humiliation that I would be forced to endure would be followed by a period of retraining, and God was also about to show me His teachers, those He had chosen for my reformation.

The Final Blow

After I told Noline about the second adultery, we were both very tender. We needed time and space to allow God's healing balm to work in our battered marriage and wounded lives; but that time and space didn't come in the way we hoped hoped. Since I shared the pulpit with the senior pastor I'd invited to join me in the work, we took turns preaching each Sunday. It was my turn to preach on that fateful Sunday morning when I publicly declared that, for the first time in five years, "There is absolutely nothing between my wife and I. We are totally transparent with each other."

The inevitable confrontation with my former lover and the public disgrace that followed came in swift order. I had failed to learn one of the most important lessons every leader should know and

spect: we all desperately need others to help us recognize blind spots in our lives. Accountability among brethren permits weaknesses and sin to be caught early, when they can be dealt with privately, before other people are hurt. Where accountability is absent, the Holy Spirit must step in to bring a much more painful and public correction to God's children.

Facing the congregation on the following Wednesday night, I realized it was an appointment with destiny that I could no longer avoid. The sin I'd confessed in secret to my wife was now appointed to be "shouted from the housetops." When the elders exposed the truth about my past adultery, my carefully constructed wall of deceit fell in ruins around me. I was now publicly branded as a liar and an adulterer. I was uncovered, laid bare and demolished.

In my misery that night, I didn't realize it, but in that moment all my falsehoods had been stripped from me — once my pretense had been removed and the need to conceal my guilt was gone — I was finally able to step into God's grace. My flesh was crucified that night. As soon as my sin was publicly exposed before all, Satan lost one of his most powerful holds over my life. I had been "giving place" to him through my continued deceit in hiding my sin. Now my sin was evident before all, and Satan lost his most effective hold over me. The first stage, that of "uprooting and tearing down" was complete.

Now the Lord would begin the rebuilding process.

It Wasn't Easy

It wasn't easy. That night, I felt like a man who was being lynched by vigilantes. It was God who had uprooted my concealed sin of adultery and long-standing deception, but I blamed the church elders. It would take the better part of two years for the scales of anger and bitterness to totally fall from my eyes, two years before I could finally admit that the leadership of the church was not the problem, two years for me to admit that my problems were caused by my own failure. It would take even longer for me to actually begin to live without using deception.

Without my knowing it, God had already fashioned a custom-made cleanup program for my life, and I had already met the "manager" of my spiritual reconstruction program. I would be biblically restored under the strong hand of Mike and Marilyn Phillipps, the very instruments God had used to help me finally confess my sin to Noline.

God sent ravens to feed His prophet in times of drought; He had angels protect His disciples in times of danger; and He had Mike and Marilyn, who now became our source of refuge and healing. In the weeks following that painful Wednesday night, I continually thought that every thing and everyone else but me had caused the problems in my life, but the Phillipps would take me to task again and again on these issues. We spent hours on the phone with them, as they gave us direction in our shattered lives. A major part of my healing and our restoration was a constant check and balance by our overseers and friends. I now know they were literally God's hand extended to two wounded people.

The most amazing part of the grace of God in our crisis is that He reached down and rescued *me*. I could understand that He would look after His prophets and apostles, but it was incredibly hard to understand why He would make provision for a "nobody" who had been a constant failure in life, while deceptively portraying outward success to everyone else. I pray that the account of mercy and grace Noline and I are sharing will reassure you that God's grace is extended to all of His children — including *you*, if you will humbly seek Him.

NOLINE:

After that Sunday service, the "other woman" confronted Neil, and he confirmed that he had told me about their affair. She immediately went to the senior pastor, and that Thursday Neil and I were called to an elder's meeting to be confronted with these allegations. I was glad that I had revealed to Neil the word the Lord had given me for him. I told him, "Neil, this is the Lord's doing. Don't defend yourself. Just remain silent throughout the whole proceeding." We did this, even though it was a humiliating and shameful experience. Everyone was looking at my husband, knowing that he had been unfaithful, and I hated to think what they were feeling toward him. Was it disgust and contempt? Or did they simply feel shame and unbelief? All I knew was that we were going to face the consequences of this sin together.

My only consolation was knowing that God was in charge. By the following week, Neil had been publicly exposed, both in the Sunday morning service and at the Wednesday evening meeting. He was crushed that he was out of the ministry he loved so much, and he was under severe discipline. He was no longer allowed to sit in the front row. He had to find a place in the congregation, a great humiliation for both of us.

It was so difficult getting up the next Sunday morning, knowing we would have to face all those people again with their stares and obvious discomfort in having to talk to us. What could they say? How were they to respond to us? It was so uncomfortable and horrid that I felt like we had leprosy! Our children did not know what had happened; they only knew that their Daddy was agonizing over some unknown problem. The Lord reminded me again and again that it was His doing, and it was His will to crush Neil, so that, as the Master Potter, He could put this now softened and pliable clay on the turning wheel in preparation for the remolding process.

My counsel and advice to all woman who have doubts or suspicions about their husbands is to go to the Word of God. Ask God to give you a "faith vision" for your husband. Ask Him to show you how He sees your husband, what His point of view is. Then write down what God tells you, and believe His report — despite the circumstances. Stand on the Word and allow God to do His complete work in your husband. This will be your strength — even if your world seems to come crashing down all around you.

NEIL:

In the days ahead, I had opportunity to examine my past life in detail. One of the things I discovered that seemed to help explain why I had fallen a second time was that I had not really been sorry for my sin, only sorry that I had been caught in it. The Apostle Paul wrote to the Corinthians:

*For though I made you sorry with a letter, I do not repent, though I did repent: for I perceive that the same epistle hath made you sorry, though it were but for a season. Now I rejoice, **not that ye were made sorry**, but that ye **sorrowed to repentance**: for ye were made sorry after a godly manner, that ye might receive damage by us in nothing. For **godly sorrow worketh repentance*** *not to be repented of: but the sorrow of the world worketh death.*

2 Corinthians 7:8-10 KJV

Like countless offenders before me, I had tried to use *remorse* or *sorrow* to win freedom from my indwelling sin. I was genuinely sorry that I was caught. I was even sorry that the adulteries had occurred. I was sorry that I had wounded so many people along the road, but I had to learn the hard way that *remorse is not enough* because it doesn't bring freedom! Sorrow has to lead to true *repentance*. When repentance is left out of the picture, you are left in a state of forgiveness, without the power to walk out of your imprisonment. Therefore, you are often doomed to sin again.

The Scriptures declare:

Repent, then, and turn to God, so that your sins may be wiped out, that times of refreshing may come from the Lord.   Acts 3:19 NIV

Suddenly, it began to dawn on me that what God had asked me to walk through in this "breaking" process were the iron bars *of my own imprisonment*! It was no wonder that I had seen no "breakthrough" with the Lord. My own refusal to repent had made me nothing but a forgiven prisoner who was still in a cage. Somehow I knew that when I finally did it God's way, even though it was the most difficult walk

walk I would ever take, I would finally be free! I hadn't yet realized that His plan involved the process of crushing and breaking — to bring me to true repentance. Only then could I begin to walk out of the jailhouse of my own making.

For years, I had preached countless sermons on godly repentance, but up until this point, I had never moved beyond my head knowledge of the subject. Now I was learning "first hand and close up" that repentance involves more than admitting wrongdoing. Godly repentance requires an abhorrence of sin, and a 180° turn away from that sin. God now demanded that I live out a repentant life-style.

I was amazed by the depth of God's grace. Although I had tried to avoid Him, deceive Him, and had even lied to His people, I now found myself walking on a pathway leading to life after a rescue orchestrated by God Himself! He had even chosen the players to work His salvation into the deepest recesses of my life. He had heard my desperate pleas for mercy, and had rescued me from my own weaknesses. What a wonderful God we serve! I give Him all the praise and glory.

We Move to Colorado

The Phillipps agreed to supervise the year of discipline we had been required by the leaders of our church to observe. That meant we had to sell our home and move to Colorado. Shortly after Noline and I were "stood down" from the ministry in 1987, we went out to join the Phillipps in Colorado for healing and desperately-needed personal ministry.

There was no guarantee of finances, and I would need to look for a job once we arrived in the United States. As it turned out, we helped to remodel the basement in the house next door to the Phillipps. Once it was completed, the upstairs of the house became our residence, and the basement housed the ministry office for the next two years. Then, so that we would not have to find a secular job, the Phillipps incorporated us into their office staff. There, we learned many new procedures and moved from total computer illiteracy to being capable of inputting data. If only my reeducation had been as easy!

Sympathy Vs. Empathy

I went to Colorado thinking the Phillipps would be sympathetic friends who would side with me in my miserable plight. Their attitude was far different than I had imagined. I discovered that although they truly loved Noline and me, their point of view on our healing was very different from mine. Everything I would try to "justify" or "play down" in the Phillipps' presence was challenged, and that is just what I needed. I had never known anyone who would take the time to challenge everything that I did. I considered their approach to be like the dif-

What is the difference between the two? If you walk into your kitchen after hosting a dinner party, and see dishes stacked to the roof, *sympathy* will say; "Oh honey, I'm so sorry that you have all those dishes to do! I'll stand here and sympathize with you, because I really do feel bad that we don't have a dishwasher." *Empathy,* on the other hand, will say, "I'll tell you what, move over! You wash, and I'll dry. Before we know it, the job will be done." Empathy, as a word, means to put your self in someone else's place, to feel what they are feeling; and, as a spiritual concept, is *becoming part of the solution* to a brother's problem.

Discipleship

That first year was to become the "school of discipleship" that we had never had in the past. It was conducted by people who really loved us and were willing to persevere with us, even though I pushed them to the limit. They were different than anyone to which I had previously related, though, and it took time for me to fully trust them in certain areas.

One of these areas was relationships to authority figures. In the past, I had gotten a huge knot in my stomach every time I was called to go over to the senior pastor's office for a visit. I had no idea what was coming and it upset me and finally resulted in an ulcer. The first few times I heard Mike's voice yell across to my office, "Neil, come here into

voice yell across to my office, "Neil, come here into my office," I felt that old familiar knot tighten inside of me. Reluctantly, I put down what I was doing and went to his office, fearing the worst. Once I stepped inside the door, however, he would invariably say something like, "Sit down. What do you think we could do here in this city?"

I could not believe that Mike was soliciting my ideas instead of coming down on me for doing something wrong. What a welcome change! I was to discover that this attitude was typical of Mike Phillipps. Slowly, I began to trust him. He and Marilyn loved us, and it showed in the good times, and also in their rebukes, correction, and instruction. I have always appreciated their commitment to being frank and transparent in their dealings with others. Their motto is, "What you see is what you get." There were no secret closets with them, and they would tolerate none from us either.

Real relationships are forged and fashioned in the fire, on the anvil of life. So it is with godly character, the fiber that God uses to truly build His Kingdom. Unfortunately, although there were many good deposits of "giftings" in me that kept me going for a long time, I had very little fiber or godly character in me. When I was under the gun, I constantly "justified" my actions, instead of taking responsibility. I also played down my true feelings, whenever I was confronted about those who had hurt me. For example, I might say to Mike and Marilyn, after a spot, "Well, you should see what *they* have done!" Yet, each time, the Phillipps would bring me back again to the real crux of the matter: God was dealing with *my sin* — not the sins of the senior pastor, the pastor's wife, or other church leaders. I deeply appreciated this necessary discipline. As the Scriptures show us:

> *Our fathers disciplined us for a little while as they thought best; but God disciplines us for our good, that we may share in His holiness. No discipline seems pleasant at the time, but painful. Later on, however, it produces a harvest of righteousness and peace for those who have been trained by it*
>
> Hebrews 12:10-12 NIV

So, discipline is tough, and the process is painful, but the product is peace and righteousness. I deeply longed for both, though I thought, at times, I would never survive the process. The real issues in my life were on the anvil, and not by my choice. My state can best be described by the words Jesus spoke to His faltering disciples in the Garden of Gethsemane: *"The spirit is willing, but the flesh is weak"* (Matthew 26:41).

The hand of God had placed me in His fiery forge of purification. I would allow His fire to burn away my impurities, and His hammer to pound out of me every imperfection that was not in line with His Word and His destiny for my life. I knew He would not relent until I could finally lay the past to rest, once and for all. He would persist until He had formed the image of His own Son deeply within my character. He was determined to lovingly place the bonds of real love and godly character within me, to keep me strong and secure in my marriage covenant to Noline. It was with this slow and painful process that God began to produce the righteous life of His Son in me.

The prophet, Hosea, revealed God's threefold plan to bring His errant children back to their inheritance in Him:

> *Come, let us **return** to the Lord. He has torn us to pieces but He will heal us; He has injured us but He will bind up our wounds. After two days He will **revive** us; on the third day He will **restore** us, that we may live in His presence.*
>
> Hosea 6:1-2

The First Season: Let Us Return

I see in this passage three seasons involved in the process of restoration. As Noline and I began to walk through these three seasons together, under the godly direction of Mike and Marilyn, our suspicions were confirmed. The first season of repentance, when we would return to the Lord, was the hardest. We had to endure the crushing, to produce the godly sorrow that in turn leads to true repentance.

All of us have two choices when we are faced with the discipline or pruning of the Lord. We can go the route of obedience and respond quickly to the Holy Spirit at His first prompting, or we can do things the hard way — like I had always done. Yielded hearts are chastised, but hard hearts must be crushed to bring deliverance. As true sheep of His pasture, we must come to repentance. Although I had spent most of my adult life searching for "another way," I had finally come to realize that God will have it done only one way — the way He has laid down in His Word.

The Second Season: He Will Revive Us

Once I finally turned around and headed back to the Lord by the power of the Holy Spirit, He began the reviving process. This is when "spring comes into full focus and the winter is over." In my own life, new buds of life and shoots of flowers soon-to-be began to spring from scarred branches that were long thought dead and lifeless. Fresh sprigs of new growth sprang up from the now broken and moistened earth of our hearts. Best of all joys and delights, we began to sense the sweet fragrance of the Spirit of the Lord once again!

Can Lazarus who died live again? Will Aaron's rod ever blossom anew with almond buds? Absolutely! Jesus said, *"I Am the Resurrection and the Life"* (John 11:25). We knew we would live again, and we

but to our marriage as well. When given the chance, the Lord will revive worship in your soul, a fresh love for the Word, and new love and affection for your spouse and the people of God. He was even birthing a new love in my heart for the "tools" He had used to bring about my downfall.

The Third Season: He Will Restore Us

In the third season of our healing, Noline and I were to taste the sweet fruit of God's long-term goal for our lives: He was going to restore us! That which the devil had stolen through my sin, rebellion, and deception, God was now able to give back to us. The devil had to pay back to us sevenfold for everything he had stolen. Restoration may mean we will be allowed to return to the work and calling we did prior to our sin, or it may not. The key is surrendering our future to Him and trusting Him for the resurrection He desires.

We now had a purpose, and we had a direction. By this time, I was willing to accept anything the Lord put into our path. Slowly, we began to make a new life for our family. Through the support of many loyal friends, friends who invested in our lives for the next two years, we not only survived — we began to grow.

Does it happen overnight? Absolutely not. God would invest in us as much time as it took to complete His work. He intended to plant the principles

plete His work. He intended to plant the principles of a new walk so deeply within me that they would last me a lifetime!

If there is one thing about which I am confident, it is that if you surrender yourself to God — no matter what your circumstances or mistakes — your future will always be better than you had before you surrendered to Him. God is for you, one hundred percent! When you have missed God's "Plan A" for your life, you are not relegated to plan B, or C, or D. No, God just creates a new "Plan A" — if you continue to do things His way and not your own. These three seasons of healing have one major purpose: to restore us to His presence. He wants us to live in His Presence and enjoy Him to the fullest.

Nothing is more devastating to a Christian who has known the presence of God than to feel he or she can no longer go back into the throneroom of grace because of sin. If I can imprint anything into your heart, it will be this fact: God loves you, and He longs to have you in His company. Your sins *have* separated you from Him, but He desires to draw you back to Himself through His process of restoration, by His Word. Respond now, today. Return to the Lord and His presence.

We had experienced crushing humiliation, and now we were experiencing caring rehabilitation.

Chapter 11

Refilling the Jars

*Nearby stood six stone water jars, the kind used
by the Jews for ceremonial washing, each holding
from twenty to thirty gallons. Jesus said to the
servants, "Fill the jars with water"; so they filled
them to the brim.*　　　　　John 2:6-7 NIV

NEIL:

Just as with the young couple in the Bible, Noline
and I began our walk of discipleship and healing in
our marriage with Jesus, at the wedding in Cana of
Galilee. As we began to earnestly seek God for healing and direction, we were led to this passage in the
Gospel of John.

God told us to pour the water of the Word into
the now empty vessels of our lives. Water, in its pure
form, is tasteless, odorless, and colorless; and that
was exactly what the "water of the Word" was like
to us when we first began to read and pray. But we
kept reading and praying anyway, even though the
Word seemed empty. At first, we didn't see anything

happening; nothing seemed to be changing.

The Water Jar of Obedience

Despite the apparent lack of results, we felt it was important to remain obedient. Jesus told the servants, at the wedding in Cana of Galilee, what He wanted them to do, and they were obedient — although they must have felt pretty foolish pouring water into those large vessels.

God is in charge of the supernatural, but He expects us to do our part in the natural. Many in the Body of Christ are conditioned to go to the altar to have hands laid on them, hoping for some miraculous healing to manifest. God does indeed heal, but He also demands that *you* do something. He expects each of us to be obedient to what He has shown us. So, every individual needs to hear from God, for him- or herself, and know what God wants him to do. For Noline and me, it was to submit to Mike and Marilyn Phillipps and the direction they would give us. And we were to get back into daily devotional reading and prayer together. Frankly, it was a relief to be able to do "something," because at that point in our lives, we were feeling pretty useless.

More than useless, sometimes I got the idea that we were going backwards. I began to feel like Mike was picking on me for minor infractions, or for how I perceived things, and I hated it. I balked at his confrontation of my attitude and my constant blaming of others. I resented the constant accountability that God had thrust into my life.

Character formation requires a surrendering of all that the flesh has valued and protected, and I had years of experience to overcome. Moreover, the Word of God didn't seem to be applicable to my daily life, didn't seem to answer my immediate problems. As we look back, however, it is clear that God was at work. He knew what we needed most in those hours and our *"empty stone water jars"* were being filled once again, slowly but surely.

God wants those of us who are wounded or broken to be healed more than we want it ourselves. The truth is that we don't know how to begin filling our empty vessels on our own. Life apart from God's healing is like living in a house with a huge gaping hole in the side. It lets in all kinds of bugs and bad weather. The first thing to do before you move in is to fix the hole. You can't start buying carpets, drapes, wallpaper, and pictures until after you have fixed the real problem. If you don't fix the hole in the wall, then all the other items you buy to beautify the house will get spoiled.

Most people who approach relationship building make the same kind of mistake: they try to beautify their relationships by fixing or dressing up superficial issues without first fixing the gaping holes. No matter how many times they try to beautify a broken relationship, everything always gets spoiled because of the more important gaps they've ignored or overlooked. You have to let God repair the gaping wound first, and only then can the rest of the details come into focus. He will use the most unusual people and circumstances to bring it about. The Bible says, *"The steps of a good man are ordered of the Lord"* (Psalm 37:23 KJV). God has specific people and places in mind for you. Let God be God and totally yield to His work in your marriage and family.

The Water Jar of the Word

God then gave Noline and me a very clear word about character reformation and the "cultivation" of righteousness in our lives through Isaiah the prophet:

> *Your silver has become dross, your choice wine is diluted with water ... . You will be ashamed because of the sacred oaks in which you have delighted; you will be disgraced because of the gardens that you have chosen. You will be like an oak with fading leaves, like a garden without water. The mighty man will become tinder; and his work a spark; both will burn together with no one to quench the fire.*   Isaiah 1:22, 29-31 NIV

This was God's way of showing us what had

happened in our lives, and how we could prevent it from happening again. Our silver had become dross, and our wine was diluted. The godly righteousness I had walked in and enjoyed as a young Christian had become contaminated by the world's ways, and by the unresolved problems I allowed to fester in my life. Even worse, I had watered down God's Word (the wine) in both my own life and in my preaching. I had diluted the rich wine of the Holy Spirit with a growing influx of polluted waters from my uncontrolled lusts. When you water down the wine of God, you dilute your very life and become spiritually impotent. I had *"a form of godliness,"* but denied *"the **power**"* of it (2 Timothy 3:5 KJV).

I began to recognize yet another aspect of error in my life: I had begun to believe that I was a mighty oak in the Spirit, a sacred oak, a "do not touch my anointed" kind of oak. Frankly, I had held an overly-inflated view of myself. I had fallen victim to the deceitfulness of sin, and the lie of the devil. His delight is to trick us into believing we are something that we are not.

Who knows how many young pastors will fall captive to the enemy in this way this year, just as I did. The expectations placed upon ministers of the Gospel are so enormous that young and inexperienced preachers may immediately begin to live out a lie by trying to be someone they are not. The secret of avoiding this pitfall is do not trust in what you think *you* are, but rest on what *He* is. He is the Alpha and the Omega. You are simply His servant and His child, a steward. What you do not own, you cannot claim.

I began to realize that I had been disgraced because of the "gardens" into which I had chosen to sow. Galatians 6:7 says, *"A man reaps what he sows"* NIV. What garden are you cultivating? What are you nurturing in your life, your spouse, and your ministry? The Lord spoke to my heart and applied the principle in Luke 16:10 directly to my life when He said, *"If you cannot be faithful over that which is least, then you cannot be faithful over much"* PARAPHRASED. If I could not be faithful in my care and love for just one person, if I couldn't release and nurture Noline to become everything she was called to be in Christ, then how could I be faithful over the needs of an entire flock? I was finally learning what I had never been taught in Bible school: Christianity has to work at home before we can export it.

God showed me that this was a spiritual law. He can take this *one seed* of obedience and nurture in one marriage, home, and family, and multiply it over and over again a thousand times. I cultivated other people's gardens while mine was in ruins. I chose to nurture my pride rather than sow and harvest humility. I allowed humility to wilt and die in my life as I pursued my own personal agenda. I nurtured other men's wives while neglecting and despising my own wife. In the end, my lust grew into a towering plant that bore much fruit, while faithfulness to my Savior, my wife, and my call to holiness, was choked to death by weeds of neglect.

Justification was the gaudy flower prostituting itself in the midst of the garden while diminishing every other plant and flowering herb. In the end, Isaiah the prophet says, those who choose diluted wine and unholy oaks and gardens will become like a dying tree and *"a garden without water." "The mighty man"* will become like *"tinder,"* and his empty works will be the spark that lights a fire that cannot be quenched.

Later, when our season of discipline was over, Noline and I bought a home in Pennsylvania; and that passage in Isaiah became a vivid reminder of how close we had come to total disaster in our lives. The house had been held up in a probate battle, so no one had lived in it for a year nor cared for its one-and-a-half acres of grounds. You can imagine what the grass was like on that property, not to mention the overgrown hedges. We literally had to repossess the land. The flower garden was totally overgrown, and it took two years to help it reestablish itself so real flowers would have a chance to grow again. It took an unbelievable amount of work to restore its beauty.

Our marriage needed cultivating also. I was ashamed of its desperate need of repair. Both Noline and I realized that the period of restoration we had experienced in Denver, with Mike and Marilyn Phillipps, was only the beginning. It would be just as difficult to reclaim our lost ground as it was to restore the neglected property we had purchased.

That property also had a large oak tree. It seemed to be strong, but signs of decay or lack of nourishment were seen in its leaves, which had begun to fade from a lush green to a dull brown color. I could relate to that tree. I have sat in meetings and seen signs that the speaker was "dry." Before, I would usually be quick to criticize, but I am now slow to point my finger at others. I know what it feels like. People know when you do not have the anointing of God resting on your life. It does not matter if you drive a Cadillac, own a mansion, or wear $800 suits. "Things" don't prove that you are blessed, or that God is necessarily pleased with you.

The law of sowing and reaping is a universal law that anyone can utilize. An unsaved man, known for his depraved, hardened, and greedy heart, heard about the principle of tithing, and began to give ten percent of all that he made. This man began to prosper, as he reaped what he had sowed, even though he was still just as unsaved as he was before. Did tithing win him favor in the eyes of God? Absolutely not. It was just the law of sowing and reaping in operation.

The same truth applies to many Christians today. What really counts is the anointing of the Lord. The anointing causes us to grow. A man's sermon may sound good, but it may still lack the anointing that can only come from a godly garden that is cultivated and worked under the guidance of the Lord.

Man looks on the outward appearance, but God looks on the heart. The Lord is not nearly as interested in our miracles as He is in our character. If we are willing, He will lead us through whatever is necessary to produce that character in our lives. For us, it was a step-by-step process, as the Lord lovingly filled each of our empty jars.

The Water Jar Of a Faith Vision

So from now on we regard no one from a worldly point of view. Though we once regarded Christ in this way, we do so no longer.

2 Corinthians 5:16 NIV

My vision had become dim and blurred, and my faith almost nonexistent where Noline was concerned. Years of wrong thinking and the reinforcement of habit and conflict in our marriage had made me helpless to "renew" my mind on my own. I was totally out of "wine" and in desperate need of a miracle. My "stone jar" was dry, and I needed a new vision of the woman God had given me, as a mate and life partner. I needed a "faith vision."

A faith vision only comes from one Source. Realizing that fact, I went to God in prayer and said the only things I knew to say: "Lord, I know how I see Noline right now. Although she is an introvert and extremely stubborn, she is a great mother to our children. She is a very loving wife, when she wants to be; and she can be frustrating when she does not.

"Lord, I'm also frustrated because Noline does not enjoy pastoral work. Her heart is just not in it. But, Lord, I want to see her from Your perspective. How do You see her? What are Your plans for her life? I want to agree with Your will, and not my own selfish desires. Please reveal to me how You see Noline, whether it be through Your Word, prophecy, or exhortation. I am open to Your instruction."

Even as I asked the Lord for a new "faith vision" for Noline, I really couldn't believe He would actually reveal it to me. He must have chosen to overlook my weak faith, however; for, as I waited on Him, He graciously spoke to my heart about my wife. My eyes were shut in prayer, and my spirit was focused on the Lord, when the inner voice of the Holy Spirit spoke to my heart:

Noline is not like you. I have called you to be in the midst of My people. Like at a busy air terminal, you are among the people as they rush back and forth to catch different flights. Noline, how-

ever, is My special agent at the Information booth. She has the wealth of many years of study in My Word, and she has a large deposit of truth stored within her. When someone has a need of pertinent information, I direct them to her.

As I pondered this word from the Lord, I began to get excited, in anticipation of seeing this calling in action in Noline's life. It didn't take long for the opportunity to present itself. We were closing out a time of ministry with Marriage Ministries International one evening, when a woman approached us. I asked if I could help her, but she hastily said no and, instead, asked to speak with Noline. I sensed I wasn't needed and promptly moved on. When that lady left Noline, she had tears in her eyes and a big smile on her face. Wondering what had happened, I asked Noline what she had said to the woman to get such immediate results. Noline just smiled and said, "Oh, I just gave her a few Scriptures that I sensed the Lord put on my heart."

At that moment, the Holy Spirit reminded me of the "faith vision" He had given me. My eyes had been opened, and I could see clearly once again. God had given me a woman who was nearly my exact opposite, and He had done it for my own good. He didn't want two extroverts running around like wild people. He wanted a balanced team with a visionary and an anchor, a leader of the people and a healer of hearts.

The Water Jar Of Restitution

"Go back to all the places where you lived and make restitution with everyone I send across your path. This especially includes all of your family." The first time I heard those words in my spirit, I thought, *I know that can't be the Lord!* I bound every lying spirit trying to deceive me. But then I heard the same words whispered in my heart again, "Go, and make restitution."

When we have grown up in an environment that says nothing should make us "uncomfortable," the idea (and especially the act) of "making restitution" is not an appealing concept. It is, however, the best way to win freedom from past offenses and to build boundaries for ourselves around our areas of weakness.

During the year we spent in the ministry office at Denver, we had plenty of time to allow the Spirit of God to fill our "water jars" to the brim, and I can remember thinking, *We must be getting close to the top.* It was then that the Lord challenged me to this further step of obedience with the command that we go back to the cities where my sins occurred and make restitution. Up to this point, none of our family members knew why we had left the churches we pastored (other than the lame excuse we had given them at the time: "The Lord led us.").

Going back and facing them was the greatest

challenge of all. We resolved in our hearts that God knew what He was doing, and that His way was by far the best path of all — although just the thought of it hurt so much. We were learning that the pain He inflicts produces abundant life, while the pain we inflict on ourselves (which may not seem as hurtful at the time) ends in death.

When we returned to our country and our towns to make restitution, we were amazed at the gracious way we were received by our family, friends, colleagues and former congregation members. For the first time, I was able to tell the real reason we had left; and, by personally accepting the full weight of blame and responsibility for my actions, I released these friends and family members to let go of the offenses they had harbored toward the people they thought had wounded us without reason.

The Water Jar Of Transparency

There is only one cure for the life masked in self-deception: transparency. It is God's "balm of healing," but it doesn't come easily. I have a profound statement that I share as we train leaders around the country: "The more you give something away, the more you have of it." In the area of woundedness and bruising, the more we give away our testimony of the victory of Jesus, the more victory we have.

We have met folks who have had similar incidents happen in their marriage, and because of their inability to share freely, they have held onto their pain tenaciously. Thirty years down the road, they are still wounded, bruised and crippled in their "one-flesh" relationship and in their relationships with others. They have not been able to trust again, so their lives have been hindered by one suspicion after another.

I remember well our first painful lesson in transparency. We were in Denver at the time. In the past, before my sin was exposed, we had taught several groups with Marriage Ministries International, and I had basically always refused to be honest about my sin. Although I was transparent with respect to my successes, I was not transparent about any of my failures. On that day in Denver, we were attending a special meeting being given in our honor. During the previous year we had completed our time of discipline and had been restored to limited ministry. Now we were being promoted to our first position of oversight, since we had originally been removed from ministry. There were couples attending the meeting from throughout Colorado and a number of neighboring states. All I remember is that there were a *lot* of people there, something I later regretted.

Mike and Marilyn had asked us speak to the group that evening, and Noline and I had diligently prepared a seven-point pastoral sermon for the occasion. We were just about to begin when Mike stood up and said, "Neil, why don't you share with everyone about your adultery." I was taken aback. Although I had been in enough MMI meetings to know that everyone was expected to be open and honest, my turn had never come. I immediately thought of all the reasons I should not do what he was suggesting. I had always been taught that telling about your sins was one of the great "no-no's" in ministry. You could never let people know your past, or they would lose respect for you as a minister. And, if people didn't respect us, it would hinder our ability to ever lead them with acceptance and authority.

These were all the same arguments I had always used most of my adult life to hide my past failures. No wonder they were now parading themselves in full uniform through my mind. No, I just couldn't do this thing. Could I?

Within a split second I realized that I had to trust my overseers on this one. I had to dismiss all my excuses and do what was necessary. Although I had never walked this road before, God would help me, as always.

That evening, for the first time in public, as my face constantly flushed and my tongue stammered, Noline and I talked candidly about the past and about our dismissal from ministry — and why. It was the hardest and most humiliating task that had ever been required of me. I felt shame, disgust, and regret all over again. When we had finished, though, we discovered that the devil's lie was just that. Our fear of being rejected because of having sinned was in error. We were lovingly accepted by those that heard us, and that night marked the beginning of our successful journey to true release of the pain of the past.

Today, we can openly share our failures and the wonderful healing of Jesus anywhere, and anytime. We touch those memories and remember the fall, but the *pain* is gone, and the bruise is completely healed.

The Water Jar Of Deliverance

When my deliverance began, it was not at the hands of some high-powered evangelist, or in a moving praise and worship service. It came on our bedroom floor when I confessed my second adultery to Noline. Tears were streaming down our faces, as we knelt on our knees, and I asked Noline to lay hands on me and bind the spirit of lust I felt had been hounding me. She reached out and put her hand on my head. Then she said, "Devil, in the Name of Jesus Christ, who died on the cross and rose again, I bind you. I command you to loose my husband right now and go! In Jesus' name I pray. Amen." This was the first time I had ever allowed such a prayer to be prayed over me. I didn't feel any immediate results, and there was no particular manifestation.

Afterward, when my sin of adultery had been exposed in the church, and we were disciplined, the senior pastor and his wife visited me at home. They suggested that we bind any demonic activity in our lives, so we went into prayer and intercession together. They gathered around the chair where I was kneeling and prayed. God revealed to them that unclean spirits of lust, fornication, and adultery had been tormenting me. They bound those demons and commanded their hold to be broken over my life. I then asked the Holy Spirit to fill, with His love and presence, those areas of my mind and heart which had been susceptible to demonic influence. From that day onward, I was free from that particular torment.

When I was first saved, I thought the "overcoming life" referred to my own ability to suppress any fleshly tendencies, but I have learned, the hard way sometimes, that I am powerless without the Lord and that it is only His strength working in me that keeps me from sin. We have nothing to boast of in ourselves. Nevertheless, when I took authority over all demons of lust and denied them the legal right to rule my life I experienced a freedom that I had never known before.

Satan, I am sure has not given up on me. But now

his henchmen are nothing more than an external force, easily recognized and dealt with. All I have to do now is lift up my shield of faith in order to "quench the fiery darts" he sends my way.

A test of my newfound freedom came when we were working in the office in Denver. Although I had freedom, my flesh was still being retrained and I still had a long way to go with my habits and behavior problems. One day, a single woman was visiting the office, and she and I struck up a conversation. It all seemed totally innocent to me, but two people, including a brother with a recognized gift of discernment, sensed that this might be a problem, and they told Mike about it. He called me into the office and confronted me.

At first, I was shocked, but then I was even more bewildered to learn that he did not want an answer or an excuse. He was just seeking an opportunity to warn me of any possible attack of the enemy on my soul. If the devil had assigned a spirit of lust against me in an attempt to retake the territory lost over the previous year, his attempts were thwarted. The two men prayed with me, and together we resisted the devil's attack on me in Jesus' name. Everyone present sensed the evil emissary leave.

God used the incident to train me to recognize such attacks before I reacted in an inappropriate way. I have become very proactive regarding these subtle schemes of the enemy, and Noline and I now guard and protect each other consistently.

We are committed, in many other ways, to work-ing on our relationship every day, convinced of the fact that if there is to be any ministry in our lives, it must begin with the a Christian example in our own home. There is a vital promise in the book of Mala-chi where God reveals why He wants us to be one:

Has not the Lord made them one? In flesh and spirit they are His. And why one? Because He was seeking godly offspring. So guard yourself in your spirit, and do not break faith with the wife of your youth. Malachi 2:15 NIV

The Lord wants us to work at developing and maintaining the unity between us because He wants a godly seed in the earth. Although developing and maintaining unity is not easy, the end result is worth the effort required. Unity allows us to experience a synergistic power between the two of us, and God gets a godly seed in our children. Therefore, unity is God's will for every marriage.

Obedience, the Word, a faith vision, restitution, transparency, and deliverance — let God begin re-filling your jars today.

Chapter 12

Restoration to Ministry

*But we have this treasure in jars of clay to show
that this all-surpassing power is from God and
not from us.* 2 Corinthians 4:7

NEIL:

Restored Love

Noline and I still can't tell you exactly the day or
hour when the miracle we had longed for occurred,
nor can we tell you exactly how God performed it.
All we know is that it happened. We were still in
Denver with the Phillipps. We had obeyed the leading of the Lord, and allowed Him to fill us with His
Word. Both of us still felt like jars of clay filled with
water instead of wine, but this time we knew our
healing had to come from God, instead of our own
efforts.

We had done everything that was humanly possible in obedience to the Lord and were in position
for a miracle. Then the morning came when we woke

up with a profound inner knowing that *we desperately loved each other!* It was uncanny. This new love wasn't based on performance (which can be taken away or lost), or explicit trust in each other (we knew in a personal way that trust can be betrayed). There was no tangible source of this love. Noline and I just "knew that we knew" that we loved one another more than words could ever describe! It was an experience every married couple dreams about, and we knew it was a gift from God.

The Miracle Worker of Galilee had again *changed water into new wine,* and Noline and I were absolutely intoxicated with it. Unlike our previous experiences as young people, this time we were "drunk on His love," and not on the effects of mere human hormones and emotional infatuation. You can imagine how our "born again" love affair, with its ecstatic love and joy, directly affected our marriage relationship! I'm sure that Mike and Marilyn thought they had some love-sick newlyweds running loose in the office. We couldn't stop smiling! We were in love again after a desperate rescue from near death, and our fresh dip in God's wine was great! Like two thirsty desert travelers who have stumbled upon a hidden oasis, we immersed ourselves continually in the Lord's life-giving draught.

We don't want to give the impression that all of our trials or tests ended that day. Quite the opposite it true. But the miracle in our marriage marked a turning point. We had allowed the Holy Spirit to probe deeply into the cracked foundations of our marriage, our friendship, and even our individual weaknesses and character flaws. He brought to the light those hidden things that were causing our foundations to crumble. He repaired the cracks in our cisterns so that they could be filled anew with the Lord's wine. Best of all, the Lord taught us how to combat the attacks of the devil through the Spirit of God instead of yielding to the dictates of the flesh.

Paul told the Corinthians that God put His treasure in human *"vessels of clay"* to show that the miracle of *"Christ in us"* is a work of God, and not of man. In other words, He planted His miraculous love and grace in flawed human beings *on purpose*, so that no man would get the glory — only God.

The same holds true for the miracle of restoration. Noline and I occasionally have times of "intense fellowship," where we lose our tempers in a moment of conflict and trade painful statements. When these times come, we, like everyone else in marriage relationships, have to trudge through the process of confession, repentance, and forgiveness to repair the temporary breaches in our relationship — so they won't become permanent.

And some of the old wounds still rise up every once in a while. This is one of the hazards of which all couples must be aware, but especially those who have experienced serious breaches in their relationship in past times. At times, when Noline and I are introduced to someone with the same first or last name as the individuals with whom I committed adultery, I see Noline make an involuntary grimace or facial contortion. This is a telltale sign that an old wound has been bumped again.

Like most couples, we also know there are certain phrases or reactions that will earn an unmistakable "glance of disapproval" if used in mixed company. These silent signals say, "You've done it again! You've gone too far." Will this extra sensitivity to things that remind us of the past ever go away? I'm not sure. Perhaps they are not supposed to. Maybe God leaves these planted in our minds as beacons of warning, like a lighthouse perched over treacherous rocks. I know we are still talking about the mistakes of David and Bathsheba, after many centuries. By comparison, though, Noline and I have reached a place of peace where the only thing that really matters is the miracle God performed to bring us back together. By His grace, we are committed to work on our relationship under the three "D"s of a successful marriage: "*Daily Dogged Discipline.*"

Noline and I were delighted to see that the new love God planted in our marriage in Denver only continued to steadily grow between us. At first, we were afraid it was just a temporary thing, but when God does a work, it has the roots of permanence in it. All it needs to prosper is continual obedience and faith. Perhaps the greatest factor contributing to our blossoming love and progress was that we were in an environment that encouraged growth. In many ways, Noline and I were enjoying a "greenhouse" growth spurt, because we were working in close proximity to people who loved us and were willing to help foster that growth.

Another part of the miracle was that my thinking had completely changed. I didn't notice it at first. I believe the Lord changes us little by little. Then, one morning we wake up with a totally new perspective. I believe the Lord often works in "cycles," to renew our minds and reform our habits and thinking. At times, we may feel we will explode with all that He has done for us; and, at other times, we feel as dry as a withered leaf in the hot sun. Now I think I understand, in some small way, how the Apostle Paul felt when he told the Colossians, *"To this end I labor, struggling with all His energy, which so powerfully works in me"* (Colossians 1:29 NIV).

Restored Spirits

God's healing work continued in us. Our year of restoration under the supervision of the Mike and Marilyn was just that — restoration. Many people think that the best way to "restore" someone who has failed or fallen into sin is to "separate, punish, and permanently mark them." But God has a much better idea: He puts us under His blood, washes us in His Word, and restores us in His tender mercy and grace. Somehow, Mike and Marilyn Phillipps got the message and decided to apply it through the anointing of the Holy Spirit.

While they were unyielding when it came to demanding honesty, pure motives, and obedience to God's Word and Spirit, they also knew that healing requires that balance be restored where it is lacking. As a dedicated workaholic, I have to confess that being restricted to working only from "8 to 5" Monday through Friday, with weekends off, was like having a second honeymoon.

I discovered that yelling and jumping in Mile High Stadium with 70,000 other fanatic Denver Bronco fans was an important part of "becoming human" again. If that was punishment, then I would like to sign up for "ten lashes" of the same kind again. At times, Noline and I thought, *If skiing at Dillon and Breckenridge was part of our punishment, then maybe we won't mind never ministering again.* I was learning that the wonderful grace of the Lord overwhelms our weaknesses and fears in His love.

*Or do you show contempt for the riches of His kindness, tolerance and patience, not realizing that **God's kindness leads you toward repentance?***

Restoration to Ministry

Romans 2:4

Most of my early experiences in the Christian life taught me (wrongly) to believe that God was always harsh, and so terribly just, that I would have to pay back all my wrongdoing with hard labor and a dutiful amount of sorrow. It was a new learning experience to be on the receiving end of His abundant but undeserved grace. He surely required genuine repentance and obedience, but just as surely He flooded us with unmerited grace and tender mercies.

Restored Ministries?

It was while we were still enjoying the euphoria of our "new lease on love" that we began to hear some disparaging remarks from past associates and friends concerning the possibility of our ever returning to full-time ministry. Some of them were saying that since I had committed adultery more than once, I had forfeited any right to public ministry.

As for us, we were not yet thinking seriously about returning to ministry at that point, but these negative remarks took us aback nonetheless. We were still recovering and weren't prepared to be declared unfit for the work of God's Kingdom.

Despite our progress in other areas, the negative comments of friends and associates concerning our future gradually began to have their affect on us.

While we were still too recently removed from the battle to consider immediate ministerial plans, we nevertheless had maintained hopes and distant dreams. Now they were taking a terrible beating. Today I recognize that those negative comments were used by the devil to plant a seed of continual unworthiness in our hearts. He hoped to seal our fate keep us right where we were, preventing further spiritual development, and depriving those who now face "like afflictions" of the benefit of our experience and the solutions we'd discovered. We swallowed the accuser's bait — hook, line, and sinker.

It is not unusual, when you have sinned against your family the way I did, for the Enemy to make you think you will never recover what was lost, or be able to live as you did before it happened. The fact is that the sin and betrayal did happen, and that fact will follow you to the grave.

King David is a good example. He was forgiven for his sin with Bathsheba, and God removed the shame and reproach from his life. But nothing could ever remove the memory of the sin and the pain it caused from his mind. That memory remained. As with many, my most difficult battle was the fight to forgive myself. It was easy to hear others say, "You're forgiven," but I struggled to really believe it in my own heart. So, when others suggested that we were unworthy to ever be used of God again, I had to

Restoration to Ministry

God Calls Us Back to Ministry

We continued our days as usual, feeling totally content to work in the office for Marriage Ministries International for as long as they needed us. Then, early one morning, as we were sharing our prayer time and devotions together, Noline suggested, "Neil, why don't we ask the Lord what He wants for our lives?" So, as we prayed, we told the Lord that if it was His will that we just do office work for the rest of our lives, we would be quite happy doing that. Personally, I felt, after experiencing years apart from God's healing presence, it would be enough for me just to be in right relationship with Him for the rest of my days.

Toward the end of our prayer time, Noline opened her Bible and felt impressed by the Holy Spirit to start reading in the Book of Corinthians:

Therefore, since through God's mercy we have this ministry, we do not lose heart. Rather, we have renounced secret and shameful ways; we do not use deception, nor do we distort the word of God. On the contrary, by setting forth the truth plainly we commend ourselves to every man's conscience in the sight of God.   2 Corinthians 4:1-2 NIV

That entire passage of Scripture exploded in our

hearts that morning. It was a *rhema,* specific word from God's *Logos* Word, illuminating our minds on the subject we had been asking God about in our prayer. The Lord was showing us that through His mercy — not educational degrees, political favoritism, or personal piety — that we would once again have a ministry.

The second part of the *rhema* in that verse was an exhortation from the Lord: *"Therefore do not lose heart."* The Holy Spirit made this so real to us that we wept together over the love God was extending to us, knowing that we were totally unworthy of it.

The third part of the *rhema* concerned renouncing *"secret and shameful ways."* There had been sins in the past that we tried to hide from each other, and even from God. We had learned to renounce those and this learning process was releasing the mercy of God for us personally. That day, we renewed our commitment to be transparent at every level and on every occasion, knowing we had tapped into a fountainhead of truth.

We were so excited about what God had shown us that day that we could hardly contain ourselves! He loved us and would again use us for His glory.

Releasing the Mercy of God

Once this *rhema* from God had burned into my heart, I was like a drowning man clutching at a life-line thrown to me by a rescuer. "Could it be so simple?" I asked the Lord.

His reply was instant, showing me that I had already crossed the greatest hurdles. He said: "The hard part is not the release of My forgiveness or mercy, but to get the man within you to be honest and to repent. If you can confront your wrong directly, face to face, give up justifying yourself, and honestly admit your shortcomings, I will cleanse, forgive, justify, anoint, and fill you with power."

I knew then that I had come a long way and that I could help others to make progress, as well. I could now teach every man that God has always loved them, but that He cannot and will not bless the sins they harbor within. Any sin we try to hide will separate us from Him, just as Adam's sin did. Only God's mercy can make us free and enable us to bless others.

I was ecstatic with joy over what God had spoken to us (and to me in particular) that morning. But I had a big problem: How could I convince our past associates, spiritual overseers, and peers that we were ready for ministry? Would they see this as "Neil trying to justify his actions again so he can get back into the limelight?" Obviously, we could do nothing to convince them ourselves. We would have to trust the Lord to confirm our new direction to others by His Holy Spirit. His Word rose up in my spirit:

Trust in the Lord with all your heart and lean

*not on your own understanding; in all your ways
acknowledge Him, and He will make your paths
straight.*   Proverbs 3:5-6

Walk In Truth

After we committed the problem of communi-
cating our newfound freedom through God's grace
to the Lord, the Holy Spirit revealed to us the key to
the solution in the First Epistle of John: Our com-
mendation to *every man's* conscience would be our
ability to *walk in truth*:

*My little children, let us not love in word or in
tongue, but in deed and in truth. And by this we
know that we are of the truth, and shall assure
our hearts before Him. For if our heart condemns
us, God is greater than our heart, and knows all
things. Beloved, if our heart does not condemn
us, we have confidence toward God.*

1 John 3:18-21

We would have no masks, no walls of deceit, but
only the truth. The truth about my past was that I
had sinned, not only once, but twice, and that I kept
that sin hidden for five and a half years. Now I could
speak of my former overseers and those who condemned me and openly acknowledge that no one
was to blame for my problem but me. Over time,
my character was being rebuilt, and now I could

proclaim the truth the Lord had me walk out on the human level in total transparency before friend and stranger alike. He would have nothing less than total obedience.

The other level of truth is at God's level. Jesus asked His Father, in John 17:17, *"Sanctify them [His disciples] through Thy truth: Thy word is truth"* (KJV). God's Word is Truth, and He requires us to walk in His truth, which is to walk in the Word. If the Word of God says, "Jump," we are to jump. If it says, "Run," we are to run. It became that simple for me. And, this time around, I was going through a much tougher school of ministry and the Word, with godly checks and balances keeping me on track. It was a winning combination that would not fail. God had promised:

> *But if we walk in the light, as He is in the light, we have fellowship with one another, and the blood of Jesus, His Son, purifies us from all sin. If we claim to be without sin, we deceive ourselves and the truth is not in us. If we confess our sins, He is faithful and just and will forgive us our sins and purify us from all unrighteousness.*
>
> 1 John 1:7-9 NIV

As I agreed to walk in the light and allow my faults to be openly revealed and confessed, I was freely forgiven and released. I began to understand that I could then openly confess, "I am washed, and I am cleansed. I will no longer allow the past to condemn me!" The work of the Holy Spirit in our lives was more than a one-day experience we could tell others about. Noline and I knew it would be a lifelong process. God wanted us to actually walk out our new life of transparency on a daily basis. Moments of transparency may come to many, but a lifestyle of transparency is much harder to find and maintain. It requires a daily death to self that most of us avoid, whenever possible.

My flesh had been trained for so long to hide behind walls of deceit that it would take time to renew my mind and reform my habits. I had now been graced with a fresh commitment and a fresh revelation from God. I also knew, however, that, most of all, I would need to be patient and give the Holy Spirit the time it would take to work out all His will in us. He was determined to teach me how to live by the Word of God through moment-by-moment obedience. Each new principle the Lord gave me would be like another railway tie laid in place beside those before it. Each new tie would become the foundation for the new pathway the Lord had ordained for us.

Will I fall again? No one has asked themselves that question more than we have. I cannot judge now, without stepping into presumption; but I know I have been forgiven and changed. I have openly ac-

knowledged my weakness and set in place boundaries and checks and balances to help me avoid the
pitfalls of the past. With the boundaries now in place,
every new fiber in my being believes I will indeed
say a resounding "No!" to temptation when it comes
knocking. Now that I know I am weak and vulner-
able in myself, I no longer trust my flesh. I can be
strong only in the Lord.

Checks and Balances

I am not "out of the woods," by any stretch of
the imagination, but I can feel the Master's hand in
mine. With the miraculous new birth of our love for
one another came a new wisdom and humility that
I had never known before. I took the opportunity,
during our time of healing, to put in place some
checks and balances for our marriage. In other
words, I made myself and my actions accountable
to certain people we knew we could trust.

The first check and balance is Mike and Marilyn
Phillipps. We are "lifers" with them and Marriage
Ministries International. Mike and Marilyn have a
direct line of communication into my life, and both
Noline and I relate with them constantly, as we work
together in the ministry.

The second check and balance is our church, and
specifically our church leadership. Our pastor
knows us, and we fully submit to his authority and

that of the elders of the church, a security I had never really enjoyed before. Accountability brings me great peace and security, though I used to fear it as limiting and "for the less mature." No man is worthy of leading others who doesn't know how to be led and instructed himself.

The third check and balance is perhaps the most important one in my life: it is Noline. In the past, I shut her out of my life, but now she has total access to me and my actions. I have given her very specific and unlimited permission to touch any area of my life that she likes. She knows me better than any other human being on earth, and she manages to love me in spite of it! My commitment to her and our one-flesh marriage relationship even comes before our children and the ministry. My failure to do this early in our marriage contributed greatly to the problems that engulfed and nearly destroyed our home and ministry.

Singleness of Heart

As Noline and I followed the Lord through each step of healing and truth, we felt the release from the Lord to go on into full-time ministry. We submitted our revelations and proposed reentry into the ministry to those who were directly over us for added counsel and confirmation. They agreed that, in the Lord's timing, and through His guidance, we should pursue ministry. This revelation of the mercy of God deeply humbled me. Here I was, a man who had betrayed so many and caused others to falter in their relationship with God, now chosen to bear His love to other marriages.

Paul wrote to the Ephesians:

Servants, be obedient to them that are your masters according to the flesh, with fear and trembling, in singleness of your heart, as unto Christ.
Ephesians 6:5 KJV

Noline and I both enjoyed ministering to marriages from the beginning. It provided us with a vehicle to teach, as well as train, believers in God's Word; but, in my heart, I always held onto the notion that it was just a temporary measure until we were again in pastoral work. After all, wasn't Marriage Ministries International a "para-church" ministry? I knew that such ministries were not always well accepted in the church as a whole.

While I felt confident that when the Lord released us to pursue ministry again, He naturally meant pastoral duties, but a deep love of ministering to marriages had been embedded in my heart. I knew that no man can serve two masters. I felt a hankering inside of me to preach. I loved to preach. In fact, I lived to preach the Word of God. Little did I know that this love for preaching was about to be "placed on the chopping block."

One day the Lord awakened me at three in the morning on a ministry trip to confront me with a choice. (I've often wondered why the Lord always seems to wake us up at unbelievable hours. My theory is that we're so zonked that He doesn't have to work through our arrogant flesh.) I needed to choose — His ministry or mine — one or the other. He could not flow through us effectively as long as I was double minded.

I hadn't realized what a stranglehold pastoral work had on my life. Like thousands of preachers across the nation, I too had been caught in the snare of making preaching a god in my life. As I thought about it, there was power in preaching, there was acceptance by people, and there was a certain pride. And, the Lord revealed, one of the reasons I held onto the desire to preach so tenaciously was that it represented job security to me. It was something I knew I could do, could always fall back on. This "new wine" of God that had touched our individual lives and our marriage, was about to bring me into a total ministry change.

That very night, I surrendered to the Lord my title of pastor and gave up the thought of ever going back into pastoral ministry. We would trust God in this "new wine" experience to fully guide and provide for us. He wanted to use our experience to help others who were hurting in their marriages, and so that is what we wanted, as well. How great is our God!

in this "new wine" experience to fully guide and provide for us. He wanted to use our experience to help others who were hurting in their marriages, and so that is what we wanted, as well. So, the problem became the ministry. How great is our God!

God gave us a divine commission to fight for the marriages and homes of hurting and broken people. He also called us to preserve the marriages of those who are not broken or hurting, but who are ready to do things God's way, according to His Word.

Once I laid aside that "hankering" to be a pastor and to preach, I discovered I had a new and special ability to listen to others and to receive truth from them. Before God touched my life in this way, I would always criticize the sermons I heard, feeling that it was a sacrifice to endure them and that I could probably do better. Now all that changed.

Time of Testing

Death to the flesh is extremely difficult, and I have found that the Lord always seals and tempers His work with a time of proof and testing, much like a blacksmith or metalworker must temper steel to make it strong. When Noline and I moved from Denver to Pennsylvania, we found a church home for our family and settled in to quietly work in the eastern region for Marriage Ministries International. I was sure I would be invited to preach before long. I remembered my choice to accept the Lord's minis-

church, did I stand behind the pulpit and deliver a message. Our pastor imported preachers from all over the country, but he never asked me to preach once. It seemed that every time he left town for a trip or vacation, a senior pastor would "step out of retirement" just to do the morning service.

Death to my desire to preach was so hard and ugly that I was almost tempted to take this as a personal rejection. Somehow, however, I knew the hand of God was involved in this. Since that time of surrender, we have been in many churches around the country and abroad, but not one offer to preach has been forthcoming. I guess God meant business after all!

Mentoring, God's Way

One of the greatest desires of my heart is to disciple others, to see them forge ahead in the things of God and be mightily used to fulfill His purposes. In the past, I unwittingly pursued a private agenda as a mentor. I realize now that I was discipling men and woman to fulfill *my* vision, just as I had been carefully groomed and discipled to fulfill the vision of a particular denomination, instead of God's vision. I manipulated others into believing they were doing the will of God, while all along, it was *my* will and vision I wanted fulfilled!

Many people are consumed with what they *think*

is God's will, because they think God supports every activity and function that is church related. Noline and I are thankful that now we have the joy of training others to do the work of the ministry. And we do not want the credit. It takes the burden of fleshly pride off of us, while allowing us to bless God's Kingdom in an important way. We are called to plant into others, so they can excel in whatever field God has called them to — whether it is being a homemaker or a missionary. We bring no agenda, other than God's agenda, as revealed in His Word. All the people to whom we minister are free to pursue their destiny under His anointing.

Our Present Mission

When we moved to Pennsylvania and served as the East Coast Directors for Marriage Ministries International for several years, we continued to work closely with Mike and Marilyn. At the end of that period, after talking and praying with the Phillipps, we felt it was time to head back to Denver to accept a national position with Marriage Ministries International, working even closer with our friends and mentors in this vital ministry.

The need for anointed, Spirit-led, and Bible-based ministry to marriages seems to continually mushroom. As success stories grow and prosperity spreads in our modern society, the problem of divorce, conflict, and marital infidelity grows as well — even in the Christian community. This is not a localized problem. It affects the entire world.

We are determined to reach the marriages of our generation with the Gospel of Jesus Christ, using every means and communication mode available. A godly standard must be raised up against the rising tide of divorce and remarriage among Christians. There is vital need for our story to be heard by hurting couples around the world, and the testimonies of other couples whose marriages have been miraculously restored must also be heard. God is still in the reconciliation business — especially when it concerns the life or death of a marriage and home!

Those of us who have received God's grace must take the responsibility of showing it to others. As the Scriptures teach:

> *We who are strong ought to bear with the failings of the weak and not to please ourselves. Each of us should please his neighbor for his good, to build him up. For even Christ did not please himself but, as it is written: "The insults of those who insult you have fallen on me." For everything that was written in the past was written to teach us, so that through endurance and the encouragement of the Scriptures we might have hope.*
>
> Romans 15:1-4 NIV

And we trust that this book has been a blessing to YOU. If your marriage is experiencing problems today, ***don't give up! Get help!*** Noline and I can tell you from experience that no matter how far gone your marriage appears to be, God is big enough to fix it! He knows how you feel, and He can help you restore the broken-down walls of your relationship. He can even restore the feelings of love you thought you would never experience again. After all, He is the God of miracles.

There are answers for your questions. You just have to go to the right Source for them. If you think your marriage can't be saved, just remember the two-time loser who preached righteousness while practicing adultery. Remember Noline and me, and take heart. God changed my heart and my ways. He saved our marriage, our home, and our ministry — just because He loved us, and He loves YOU just as much.

If you are one of the many thousands of people in ministry today who have been thrust into a similar arena of sin and self-justification by the same kind of character defects that I describe here, I trust that you will trust the Lord Jesus Christ to help you. Call out to Him, "Yes, Lord, that's me. Help me to yield to Your Spirit so You can build godly character into my life, character that will stand the test of temptation and allow me to say no to sin. I want to serve you faithfully, Lord, and to be a good example for others to follow. Set me free from sin and all its consequences."

Are you ready to take the first steps for your miracle? If so, let the Lord Jesus Christ begin the re-filling of your water jars today.

We leave you with the prayer of Paul for the Ephesian church. It is our prayer for you today:

Therefore I also, after I heard of your faith in the Lord Jesus and your love for all the saints, do not cease to give thanks for you, making mention of you in my prayers: that the God of our Lord Jesus Christ, the Father of glory, may give to you the spirit of wisdom and revelation in the knowledge of Him, the eyes of your understanding being en-lightened; that you may know what is the hope of His calling, what are the riches of the glory of His inheritance in the saints.

Ephesians 1:15-18

Amen!

When we completed our time of discipline and departed for Pennsylvania, Mike and Marilyn Phillipps wrote the following note to us.

How often we had seen families of those in ministry cast out because of sin, abandoned by those who could help them heal, and rejected by those whose love and support they so desperately needed. We cried out to God for the opportunity to reach into the lives of a family like that and help restore them to life. We didn't know how; we only knew Jesus was able and we couldn't bear to see one more man of God evicted, one more family rejected and alone. We prayed and God heard. And He sent you.

The excitement we felt as you arrived was only matched by the vague fear that perhaps after all that waiting for you to get here, we might fail you in some way. We knew so little of what was to be done, but we knew we couldn't leave you as you were. We knew Jesus would minister healing to His precious sheep and we trusted Him to be faithful.

How little we suspected back then how very much we would grow to love you. Jesus never told us that would happen. Perhaps He was sparing us the grief that this moment of your going would bring. You came to Denver a wounded bird whose wings were broken as badly as your hearts. Since that time we have watched you heal and strengthen; we have watched you blossom; we have watched the first stretching and flapping of your mended wings; and now we watch you soar into the distance with newfound strength and power in Him.

You were created and called to soar and so you must. You would be as uncomfortable staying put as a healed bird would be living in the nest forever. We know you must go, but a part of us goes with you. We will never be the same because of what God has done here. We know there will be many, many more families who come for healing. With each one we greet, though, we know our hearts will recall the day you arrived. As each one heals and moves on, we will always be reminded of this day, now, with you.

Satan tried to crush you and what he did not accomplish, man tried to finish. Those who carry the living God within them, though, cannot be finished. The call of God and anointing within you has triumphed! Once again you go forth ministering in His name.

With each life you touch, each victory you experience, we will rejoice. A part of you remains with us and a part of us goes forth with you. We will always be here if you need us and, in our hearts, we know you will always be there for us. Sometimes along the road of life, God allows a very special blessing to come forth from ministry. This, our dear friends, has been one of those times.

BOOKS AND TAPES THAT WILL BLESS YOUR MARRIAGE

— Books by Neil and Noline Rhodes —

Breaking Loose: Taking Your Marriage to A Higher Level of Fulfillment

Why are so many Christian marriages being destroyed? What is holding God's people back from the deeper fulfillment He intended for our marriages? Neil Rhodes puts forth the forceful argument that we have been wrongly conditioned by this world's way of thinking and that we need to develop a whole new way of thinking, God's way of thinking, before we can experience the joys He intended for marriage.

$9.00

Refilling the Jars: Finding Hope After Adultery

Is there hope for a marriage when one of the partners has fallen into adultery and betrayed his or her spouse? Can Christians be forgiven the sin of adultery? Answers to these questions are never easy, but Neil and Noline Rhodes face them head on and present practical steps that can be taken to resolve the underlying marital conflicts that often lead to adulterous relationships.

$7.00

— Tapes by Neil and Noline Rhodes —

They Have No Wine (Love), 1 tape $4.00
One Flesh 1 tapes $4.00
Intimacy, 2 tapes $8.00
Highlights, 1 tape $4.00
5-TAPE SET $16.00

The Snare of the Fowler, *1 tape* $4.00
Dealing With Anger, *1 tape* $4.00
Fighting For the Home, *1 tape* $4.00
The Greatest Investment, *1 tape* $4.00
4-TAPE SET $12.00

Building Marriages Jesus Style, *1 tape* $4.00
The Kingdom and Relationships, *1 tape* ... $4.00
The Kingdom and Influence, *1 tape* $4.00
The Kingdom and Righteousness, Peace and
Joy in Marriage, *1 tape* $4.00
4-TAPE SET $12.00

Unity of the Spirit in the Home, *1 tape* $4.00
Unity of the Faith, *1 tape* $4.00
Unity in Relationships, *1 tape* $4.00
Unity in Communion, *1 tape* $4.00
4-TAPE SET $12.00

TO ORDER, CALL OR FAX (303) 978-1722

Neil and Noline Rhodes are available to speak for churches, seminars, retreats and conventions

Please write or call:

8452 S. Upham Way
Littleton, CO 80128

e-mail: fit@power-online.net
(303) 978-1722